Power, Passion, and Purpose

PRAISE FOR ANN ROULAC'S
POWER, PASSION, AND PURPOSE

"An inspirational, resourceful and practical guide to personal power and sustainable beauty."

Angeles Arrien, Ph.D.,
author of *The Four-Fold Way*

"This is a unique compilation of spiritual and practical information for those who seek to understand their unique source of power."

Marilyn McGuire,
Nautilus Book Awards

"This caused me to stop and think how to be more efficient in the midst of a hectic work day. It reminded me to take a break and learn how to recoup my energy."

Marci Cohen,
Senior Vice President,
AFL-CIO Housing and Investment Trust

"Power, Passion, and Purpose is a primer for healthy living for anyone who's up against stress. Ann shows how to tap our own resources for the antidote that will transform our lives and the lives of those around us."

David Gazek, Senior Vice President,
AIMCO

"Ann's wonderful book is a time-tested field guide of wisdom that shows us how to achieve and maintain physical, emotional, mental, and spiritual well-being in a complex world."

Robert Rabbin, speaker,
author of *Igniting the Soul at Work*

"Ann Roulac achieves "great "kahuna" status through her book *Power, Passion, and Purpose*. She delivers secrets to healthier, better-integrated living. All leaders will learn so much from it."

John Renesch, business visionary,
author of *Getting to the Better Future*

"Ann Roulac offers a time-tested blueprint for working with energy to transform the body and all of one's relationships."

Michael Sky,
author of *The Power of Emotion*

Power, Passion, and Purpose

7 Steps to Energizing Your Life

ANN NICHOLS ROULAC

GREEN ISLAND PUBLISHING

Library of Congress Control Number: 2005937720

Library of Congress Cataloging-in-Publication Data:
Roulac, Ann Nichols
Power, Passion, and Purpose: 7 Steps to Energizing Your Life
Includes bibliographical references.
ISBN 0-9773323-2-2   (cloth : alk. paper)
1. Self-help;
Title: Power, Passion, and Purpose: 7 Steps to Energizing Your Life

Green Island Publishing
709 Fifth Avenue
San Rafael, California 94901

This book is dedicated to my mother,
Elizabeth Y. Roulac,
for her wisdom, knowledge and vitality,
who started me on my path of study
of ancient cultures, and to
the spirit of my father,
Phil W. Roulac,
for his courage and power of presence,
who taught me the art of observation.

Contents

Preface

My interest in the wisdom of the ancients—upon which this book is built—began in my teens after reading Carlos Castaneda's first book, *The Teachings of Don Juan*. His extraordinary stories of the sorcerer Don Juan Matus and his shamanic lineage, so dramatically different from the traditions of the world I lived in, forever altered my perspective—about life as well as death. We are more than we think we are, the book was telling me. Our potential is vast.

My mother, Elizabeth Roulac, greatly influenced my openness to new ideas. By the time she was three years old she had lived in three countries: Honduras, Spain, and the United States. When she was twelve, her family moved to Shanghai, China, where my grandfather, Arthur Nichols Young, served as financial advisor to Chiang Kai-shek from 1929 through 1947. The fact that she grew up in different cultures and, at the age of 89, still travels to several different countries every year, has had a significant impact on my world view.

My fascination with nontraditional ways of knowing took a startling turn while I was supervising a small staff in a large financial institution. I was your basic Type-A driven personality, and it irritated me when staff members got sick. It irritated me even more when they said they caught their flu or cold from someone in the office. I wondered why I rarely got sick. Because I was so focused on my work? Because I felt I had more control over my life? Or was it something else? Then I started to predict with accuracy who next would fall ill and for how long they would be absent from work.

Unnerved by this experience, I deepened my study of ancient traditions and healing practices, trying to understand why I was able to predict the health of others. No big answers came immediately, but years later I heard about Carolyn Myss, a medical intuitive who was achieving great success identifying illnesses without the use of conventional diagnostic tools. So I hadn't been going crazy after all!

In the late eighties I started studying with Angeles Arrien, a cultural anthropologist and one of the most articulate individuals I have known. It was from Arrien that I learned the concept of presence and "the four intelligences." She explained that we all have the capacity to develop our mental, emotional, physical, and spiritual levels of intelligence, but that Western culture has prioritized for the development of mental skills.

Many of the individuals I've worked with—employees, colleagues, and clients, most of them highly educated and holding prestigious titles—lack what we think of as intuition, inner knowing, or a sixth sense. Time and again I have watched them make poor business decisions. The reasons didn't become clear to me until I considered their decision-making skills from the perspective of the four intelligences. They simply weren't using all the tools available to them.

GETTING IN TOUCH WITH YOUR POWER

In the last thirty years I've had the privilege of working with many successful individuals who lead balanced lives and make huge contributions to their companies and communities. And yet, even though a number of them were among the wealthiest people in the world, most of them—like most of us—are not truly in touch with their own mastery and power. Success is not the result of a particular level of intelligence or education. While the benefits of a quality education and of being very smart make the journey to success a little easier, they are not the primary prerequisites for greatness. One of the distinguishing attributes of successful individuals is that they view their work as only part of their purpose or contribution.

Having spent most of my business career in the fast lane, I know that I am as susceptible as anyone to loss of perspective and the stress that follows. I've also come to know that I have the capacity to balance myself and to make wise choices, to create a state of being where I'm acting more than reacting, in control more than out of control. This enables me to concentrate on more important life issues and commitments without the discomfort and distraction of physical, emotional, and psychological distress. In fact, from my own experiences, observations, and interviews with truly successful people, I know it is possible to work, live, and even thrive in this stressful world of ours without compromising health and principles. More importantly, I believe that by developing our "shapeshifting/shamanic" potential—the ability to change and control our state of being—we tap into a deeper source of balance and wisdom that can profoundly impact how we see ourselves and the purposes we choose to follow.

We will always have personal challenges to deal with, but each problem presents an opportunity to learn and grow, and brings with it an infinite number of potential solutions. We are the only impediments to our own mastery. We are the only limitations to living a fulfilling and rewarding life and growing into our own power.

I believe that we each have a specific and important mission to fulfill in this lifetime, and that when we are not on track with our mission and purpose, we feel drained of energy, life, and spirit. When we develop a strong sense of who we are, when we begin to access our own personal power and inner wisdom, we will begin to manifest our deepest visions and dreams.

For more than 50,000 years, ancient cultures have acknowledged "energy systems" as the key to healing, mastery, and personal power. Daily practices designed to increase, manage, and balance personal and collective energies were a routine part of life for many of our distant ancestors. These practices are still around today, offering numerous benefits for anyone who wants more control over their health and more wisdom for making the right decisions.

Over the years I have been privileged to train with dynamic teachers of yoga, Reiki, Chi Gung, Tai Chi, ancient dance, feng shui, toning/ chanting, and a variety of meditation techniques. I have studied the practices of shamanism from a cross-cultural perspective, from the Native cultures of the Americas and Asia to the Celtic traditions of Europe, including Tibetan, Taoist, and Egyptian alchemy. From experience and observation, I know that the wisdom of the ancients can contribute immeasurably to the quality of our lives and the future of our planet.

It is thus my hope that *Power, Passion, and Purpose* inspires millions of people to become their own energy healers and transform their lives as well as those of their families, co-workers, and communities.

ANN NICHOLS ROULAC
Orcas Island, Washington

Change is our catalyst of growth, the trigger catapulting you
and I to new ways of viewing ourselves, through our lens
of feelings, emotions and relationships. We are asking ourselves
to move beyond the limits that we have imposed upon
ourselves, and upon one another, in the past. You and I,
individually and collectively, are determining in this
moment how humanity as a whole is to respond to change.
Will we choose grace and ease or illness and disease?
The change is happening now. It is occurring within your city,
within your family, within your body, your emotions, and your
patterns of sleep.

GREGG BRADEN
Walking Between the Worlds:
The Science of Compassion

Introduction

The twenty-first century is an especially difficult period for humanity. We live in much more complex times than those of our ancestors 35,000 years ago. Every day presents innumerable opportunities to lose our balance and sense of control. We are challenged to stay on track and keep our wits. In response, we keep shifting and adjusting, like a skier navigating uncertainly down a difficult slope. Unfortunately, we continue to have trouble avoiding the obstacles and staying on our feet.

Most people aren't adequately equipped to face the daily challenges of an accelerated lifestyle. In today's stress-filled world of speed, complexity, and uncertainty, many feel agitated or worse. Our busy lives leave no time for solitude or reflection, and whatever time we do have is usually spent seeking some kind of relief. Then, when it comes time to make important life decisions, take action, and move forward, we complain that we simply don't have the energy and often turn those key decisions over to others, either consciously or by default.

It's true that some people thrive on stress, and I have clients who jokingly claim that they're not stressed—they create stress. Some experts even say that high levels of stress are healthy. But whether you claim to enjoy the pace of a relentless 24/7 lifestyle or are finding your work and personal environment more and more oppressive, unrelenting stress will eventually wear you down.

Research shows that constant exposure to tension-producing situations shortens life spans, increases the probability of life-threatening illnesses, and diminishes everyday well-being in a variety of ways. Stress has been linked to all of the leading causes of death, including heart disease, cancer, accidents, and suicides. Between 75 and 90 percent of all visits to primary care physicians are for stress-related complaints.

What we experience as stress is actually distress, fueled by conflict, feelings of loss, unfulfilled desires, and loss of control. Such struggles drain energy that could be used in much more productive ways. How many of the following energy drainers are familiar to you?

- Chronic over-commitment—Trying to do and be everything to your colleagues, family, friends, children, parents, neighbors, or community.
- Worry—Fretting about what happened yesterday or what may happen tomorrow.
- Inertia—Holding on to relationships, jobs, and other attachments that no longer serve you.
- Judgment—Criticizing others and then obsessing about how to fix or change them.
- Low self-esteem—Worrying about what others think of you.
- Incompletion—Projects hanging over you that you've started and never completed.
- Unmet expectations—Trying to live up to others' or your own abnormally high standards.

In our fast-paced world, it's easy to settle for less, to just make do and lose sight of our purpose and passion. We sense this is happening when we feel less enthusiastic about our work or personal life. Sometimes we feel such a dip in energy that we become lethargic, apathetic, or depressed. Even when we slow down and reflect that maybe things aren't so great, we may quickly deny these feelings. We are masters at creating distractions and excuses for why we're not doing what we were meant to do.

Even though we all have the capacity to make choices that will lead to greater happiness and health and a heightened state of awareness and insight, we've been programmed to accept and follow a path of confusion, resignation, and limitation. We deny what's going on around us, using various methods to escape from or deaden ourselves to the pain. We keep giving away our power to politicians and experts while allowing media sound bites to tell us what is real and what matters in the world. Are these the inevitable consequences of modern life? Only if we allow it.

You have the choice: to feel victimized by these conditions, or to take personal responsibility to address them. You have the ability to transform your work and personal life into rewarding and satisfying experiences. You can break through, change your reality, and reclaim control of your destiny. To get there, you must be ready to let go of what isn't working and become an alchemist—transforming your inner and outer worlds while you shift from feelings of powerlessness to power. Ultimately, you must choose to be an active part of the solution.

A growing number of people are doing just that: waking up to the need to make changes in their lives and creating a wellness and wisdom revolution. At the center of this revolution are the tools of energy management and the disciplines of ancient technologies.

ACHIEVING GREATER VITALITY AND AWARENESS

Power, Passion, and Purpose explores how the four intelligences (physical, mental, emotional, and spiritual) and the four modalities of energy practice (breath, movement, sound, and stillness) can get us back in touch with our own personal power. As described in a series of seven steps, you will learn how to:

- Identify the activities and beliefs that drain you of energy.
- Increase and manage your personal energy.
- Access the higher dimensions of consciousness where healing occurs.
- Develop a strong sense of inner knowing, as if you are being guided by a universal or divine presence.
- Have greater access to creative ideas and thinking.

- Achieve a greater degree of productivity and success.
- Live a longer, healthier and more fulfilling life.

In Part One, the "seven steps to energizing your life" are presented individually. Each one explains why that step is important, offering tips for how to make it part of your daily routine and concluding with a page of bulleted "Power Notes" that summarize the key points in the section.

Part Two of the book is comprised of three sections. "Manifest Your Desires, A Guided Self-Inquiry and Action Plan" provides a self-evaluation program to help you identify what you really want in life. You will gain insight on how to re-discover your life dreams and passions and what your life purpose or life work might be. "Energy Practices" describes easy-to-learn breath, movement, sound, and stillness routines for activating a program of personal energy management that promotes greater levels of vitality and awareness. Some of the practices you will resonate with, and others you won't. Since everyone's needs are different, use only what applies to your own unique life situation. For optimal life functioning, however, it's best to incorporate some form of each modality—breath, movement, sound, and stillness—into your practices. The final section, "Words of Wisdom," is a compilation of quotes, excerpts, and prayers from some of the world's greatest teachers and spiritual leaders, designed to encourage self-reflection and to inspire a positive attitude.

The disciplines, practices, and beliefs I present in this book have been used successfully for thousands of years. I have relied on all of them at different points in my life to improve my health, my career, my relationships, and my perspective on what is possible in this world. And though I've been studying ancient cultures for over 35 years, only in the last 15 have I begun to see that the foundation of and beliefs behind all world cultures and religions are the same. These universal truths and principles have united humans for millennia and have the capacity to transform the world we now live in to one of greater harmony.

The "practice" of energy is an integral part of many of these ancient beliefs. And while some energy disciplines are taught or presented as secret rituals or the "only way" that one can achieve wholeness, most are much more open. Secret or not, though, I have come to realize that every one of them offers life-transforming results, and we all intuitively possess the knowledge of their ancient wisdom. The key is to find the practices that work for you—those that are easy to learn and that you enjoy. Additionally, you don't need to become an adept or master practitioner to achieve significant benefits. No matter which direction you choose, your life will change when you learn the principles of energy and incorporate the four aspects of energy practice into your daily life.

BECOMING FULLY ENGAGED

Power is the ability to get things done—to take action and realize your goals and dreams. Personal power is the ability to create what you want in life. When you reach a greater understanding of who you are, it gives you power. The more self-knowledge you have, the easier it becomes to create what you want rather than settling for less. If you don't have the self-knowledge, you don't have the power. If you don't have the power, you can't create what you want in life.

The process required to regain power over our lives is not for the timid. Taking the necessary steps requires a life-altering shift in your worldview. But why remain powerless when you can get in touch with who you are and gain a sense of your own personal purpose and passions—what truly makes you happy. When you align yourself with change, and flow with the pace and energy of the universe, realignment occurs. You need only to strengthen your will to live life more fully.

This book is intended to help you take the actions that will support you in becoming more engaged and energized. It explores the importance of defining one's purpose in life, and how work can become part of that journey. A personal spirituality is also vital to embracing one's life purpose; in fact, the integration of purpose, mission, spirituality, and work leads to mastery and personal power and the fulfillment of our deepest desires. When you are fully engaged and energized, you will know how powerful you truly are.

PART ONE

DISCOVER YOUR POWER, PURPOSE, AND LIFE WORK

CHAPTER ONE

The Pursuit of Power

What is needed is a realization that power without
love is reckless and abusive and that love without
power is sentimental and anemic. Power at its best
is love implementing the demands of justice.

MARTIN LUTHER KING, JR.

Most cultures identify powerful individuals as those with the greatest amount of control over others. Political and business leaders certainly qualify, but the phenomenon of power isn't limited to people in obvious positions of influence—it applies to anyone who claims a superior position as a result of race, education, net worth, physical strength, physical beauty, position of authority or accumulation of assets. Special knowledge, sexual prowess, where one lives, or who one knows can also lead to such claims.

But true power comes from within. Those who are in touch with their own true power have a presence and a quality that affects the people around them. They impress not because they want to but because of the energy they radiate, which often has nothing to do with material accomplishment or career success.

Unfortunately, many of us feel power-less and unable to make a difference in our lives or in the world. When we feel power-less we don't feel power-full, and end up wanting what we think we don't have, which we view as external to us. This is one of the reasons why we emulate the lifestyles of those we perceive as having made it. We focus our attention—sometimes to the point of obsession—on pursuing the things they have: more money, more beauty, more toys, more authority. If we can just get a bit more of that, we can control our lives and feel safe and secure.

But these are only *symbols* of power. Real power is not about control, or looking good, or having more. Real power is about getting in touch with your strengths, skills, talents, and gifts—your unique purpose and contribution to the greater whole. To reclaim your power, you need to let go of your fears of making mistakes and leaving your comfort zone, stop worrying about what others think, and open yourself to the constant flow of ideas, opportunities, and energies that are available to every one of us, all of the time.

SLOWLY LOSING CONTROL

The tendency to look outside oneself for answers is largely a product of our techno-materialist culture, spinning at breakneck speed. We're addicted to the adrenaline rush of a 24/7 lifestyle, constantly responding to crisis and chaos with hardly any time to reflect on what we're actually doing. And yet its dizzying pace makes us feel important and worthy. We've come to believe that if our time is in demand every minute of the day, if our days and nights are filled with activities, then we must be doing something right.

These distractions and perceptions can lead to some disempowering beliefs and habits. Do any of these statements sound familiar to you?

- I don't have a purpose; I've given up on my dreams.
- I don't exercise often or eat very well.
- I tend to focus on the negative, not the positive.
- I'm not very adventurous.
- I'm not very organized.
- I'm not very good at returning phone calls, letters or e-mails.
- I'm often late to meetings, appointments or engagements.

Judith Orloff, a physician, medical intuitive, and author, writes in her book *Positive Energy: 10 Extraordinary Prescriptions for Transforming Fatigue, Stress & Fear into Vibrance, Strength & Love*, that "A hidden energy crisis threatens our world. Our high-tech volatile society thrusts many of us into chronic physical, emotional, and spiritual depletion. Bombarded by information overload, burned out by enslavement to beepers, e-mail, faxes, and phones, we sink into despair. No surprise: our energy suffers. Most alarming, we've learned to tolerate tired, joyless states as normal."

And so this rutted speedway life, further complicated by new threats to our physical security, compromises our health, stretches our financial resources, and diminishes our ability to make wise decisions about our work and our relationships. When we experience the present as chaotic and the future as unpredictable, it's easy to become confused and therefore tentative in moving forward in a meaningful way. Sometimes all we want to do is hide under the covers!

In such a climate of confusion and uncertainty, when we aren't in touch with our purpose and our power, we become susceptible to the opinions of well-meaning others—family, friends and neighbors, gurus and therapists, psychics and astrologers, even the local columnist—who think they have the answers. This is especially true during times of transition, when we're stressed and overwhelmed. And so we can reach such a low point of powerlessness, such a high degree of belief in our inability to control our destiny, that little by little, often unconsciously, we give away our power until there isn't much left.

Samuel Johnson, the 18th-century writer, once stated, "Power is always gradually stealing away from the many to the few because the few are more vigilant and consistent." The easiest way to deal with our complex world when faced with too many choices and too little time is to allow others to make choices for us—the kind of mindset that the advertising industry thrives on.

FREE WILL

Every time you give away your power or your freedom to make your own choices, you diminish your vitality and your ability to live life fully. This is an important loss, because every day you make decisions both large and small that impact your life and the lives of those around you. You make decisions about your job, livelihood, or career; your significant other, family, and children; your finances and investments; your diet and your health, as well as solutions to illness and disease; foods you consume; which prescription drugs and supplements to take—the list goes on and on.

Malcolm Gladwell, author of the national bestselling book *blink: The Power of Thinking Without Thinking*, states:

> What we think of as free will is largely an illusion. Much of the time we are simply operating on automatic pilot and the way we think and act and how well we think on the spur of the moment are a lot more susceptible to outside influences than we realize.

Consider the following questions and reflect on how much control you feel you have over your life and your decisions:

- Are you always changing your mind?
- Do you frequently ask others for advice?
- Do you make your own decisions or let others do that for you?
- Who and what influence your decisions?
- Are you aware when someone is manipulating you?
- Can you stand up to dominating and controlling people?
- Do you conform to win approval?
- Are you doing what you want or what others expect you to do?

As the late mythologist Joseph Campbell once warned, "The world is full of people who have stopped listening to themselves or have listened only to their neighbors to learn what they ought to do, how they ought to behave, and what the values are that they should be living."

It's fine—even important—to seek the counsel and opinions of others, especially in areas outside of our technical expertise. But there's a fine and delicate line between being open to suggestions and learning from others— being coachable—and succumbing to control and manipulation, however subtle those influences may be. Knowing the difference will bring you one step closer to reclaiming control and accessing your personal power.

REDISCOVER YOUR INNER AUTHORITY

> Why do you bother about the Masters: The essential (thing) is
> that you should be free and strong, and you can never
> be free and strong if you are a pupil of another, if you have
> gurus, mediators, Masters over you.
>
> KRISHNAMURTI (1895–1986)
> In *The Books in My Life* by Henry Miller, 1952

As most of us would agree, going back and forth between feelings of power-lessness and seeking the wrong kind of power is not a wise way to live. Each of us knows quite naturally what's right for us; we don't need someone else to manage our personal lives and control our decisions. In *Setting Your Heart on Fire: Seven Invitations to Liberate Your Life*, Raphael Cushnir asks his readers to consider their lives and then ask themselves the following question: *Am I fulfilling my highest potential?*

From personal observation, I've concluded that those who are in touch with their personal power, who are fulfilling their highest potential and living a full life, have at least some and often all of the following characteristics:

- Know who they are, what they want, where they are going, and with whom they want to spend time.

- Are aware of their strengths, gifts, and unique qualities and what's "right" for them.
- Do what they say they are going to do and are clear about their priorities and values.
- Stay in the present, neither dwelling on the past nor worrying about the future.
- Believe in the power of something greater than themselves and/or feel guided or supported by God.
- Have a strong sense of self but are not self-centered (i.e., their life does not revolve around their needs and wants).
- Are passionate about making a difference in the world.
- Have learned to choose their battles and causes.
- Are selective in their activities and relationships.
- Don't manipulate, bully, intimidate, or try to control others, be they spouse or partner, children, parents, colleagues, co-workers, or friends.

And so instead of turning your life's decisions over to others, commit to your own empowerment and to symbols of inspiration and guidance that *you choose* to follow. Start by making a list of people whose qualities you admire, who represent the ideals you aspire to. Create a storyboard or collage of your favorite quotes and/or places that inspire you. Start a small notebook of what you want to manifest in your life and the ways you want to make a difference in the world. This will get you started. Then use the tools provided throughout this book to help turn those desires into reality.

POWER NOTES

- True power comes from within. Those who are in touch with their own true power have a presence and a quality that affects the people around them.
- When you feel power-less, you don't feel power-full, and end up wanting what you think you don't have, which you view as external to you.
- Real power is about getting in touch with your strengths, skills, talents, and gifts—your unique purpose and your contribution to the greater whole.
- We're addicted to the adrenaline rush of a 24/7 lifestyle, constantly responding to crisis and chaos with hardly any time to reflect on what we're actually doing.
- When you experience the present as chaotic and the future as unpredictable, it's easy to become confused and tentative.
- You can reach such a low point of powerlessness, such a high degree of belief in your inability to control your destiny, that little by little, often unconsciously, you give away your power until there isn't much left.
- The easiest way to deal with our complex world when faced with too many choices and too little time is to allow others to make choices for us.
- Each of us knows quite naturally what's right for us; we don't need someone else to manage our personal lives and control our decisions.

CHAPTER TWO

Your Purpose and Life Work

Every one of us has our own gift, from the agile rock climber to the "fix-it genius," to the single mother who raises three healthy kids and maintains a full-time job. It is ironic but very true that we are often the last ones in the world to be able to see and acknowledge our own gifts or areas of intelligence. Most of us are pretty blind to the things we do best.

SHAKTI GAWAIN,
The Path of Transformation:
How Healing Ourselves Can Change the World

As children, most of us dreamed about what we would do when we grew up. These dreams changed almost daily depending on our activities and our exposure to new possibilities. As we grew older, the pressure to perform—at school, in sports, in our extracurricular activities—increased. Our plans for our future became enmeshed with the desire to be liked and to please others—our friends and peers, our parents and family, even our guidance counselors—and how we would earn a living. The hobbies we pursued were often recommended to make us look good or help get us into a certain college. For most, our dreams became a distant and often forgotten memory, replaced by the realities of fitting in and getting ahead.

Those dreams may have faded, but our uniqueness never did, and that is the key to rediscovering a life purpose. We each possess our own particular genius and the ability to make a distinctive contribution to our relationships, workplaces, and communities. The more we learn and gain clarity about our special gifts, talents, and passions, the closer we will get to that experience we sought when we were younger—doing something that is uniquely ours. Rick Warren's national bestseller, *The Purpose Driven Life: What on Earth Am I Here For?*, suggests that millions of individuals are searching for greater meaning and purpose in their lives. Warren describes the metaphors in the Bible that teach us about the transient nature of life on earth and how we should remember that our lives are short-term assignments. "Earth is only a temporary residence," he writes. "You won't be here long, so don't get too attached." And yet he is quite serious about how important our short stay is. Warren goes on to say:

> You were put on earth to make a contribution. You weren't created just to consume resources—to eat, breathe, and take up space. God designed you to make a difference with your life. While many best-selling books offer advice on how to "get" the most out of life, that's not the reason God made you. You were created to add to life on earth, not just take from it. God wants you to give something back.

When you are clear about your soul's purpose in this life, you more easily become self-directed, creative, optimistic, and even joyful. When you live your life purpose, you are much less susceptible to fear, anger, guilt, or the need for approval. Your purpose provides direction and guidance; it motivates and drives your life. Materialism and the quest for more money and possessions are motivating factors for many, but such goals are not life-sustaining. Achieving them provides only temporary satisfaction; they don't feed our souls. I believe this is the main reason why many people who attain a high level of financial comfort and/or career success resort to mood-altering drugs to alleviate depression. In spite of their wealth and accomplishments, they still feel empty, as if something is missing, and the pain of that realization is too much to bear.

And so the challenge for each of us is to find that "missing" piece, to embrace our gifts and put them in service to a grander vision of who we can become and how we can contribute. Those with a clear life purpose are not as vulnerable to workplace stress and the pressures of day-to-day living. They are able to see the big picture and observe how the decisions they make either contribute—or not—to their own personal growth, the life they want to lead, and the impact they want to make on the world around them. When you integrate power, passion, and purpose—the essence of personal mastery—you can accomplish great things.

> Don't let a day go by without asking who you are. Understanding is a skill, and like all skills it must be coaxed into existence. To understand who you are means returning again and again to the question, Who am I? Each time you return you are allowing a new ingredient to enter your awareness. Every day is filled with the potential for expanding your awareness, and although each new addition may seem tiny, overall the accumulation will be great. It may take thousands of days to know who you are; it takes only one day to quit asking. Don't let today be that day.

> DEEPAK CHOPRA
> *The Book of Secrets:*
> *Unlocking the Hidden Dimensions of Your Life*

IDENTIFY YOUR LIFE PURPOSE

> When you're in your nineties and looking back, it's not going to be how much money you made or how many awards you've won. It's really what did you stand for. Did you make a positive difference for people?
> ELIZABETH DOLE

Many have not taken the time to determine what their life path or purpose might be and what they are passionate about. Since there are no courses in school to help us determine what would truly make us happy, we often end often end up taking the path of least resistance. In some cases this path may be the right choice, and we gain valuable lessons along the way. But now more than ever, it is important for all of us to be working, whether it's career or community work, in areas that truly feed our creative passions, energize us, and fill us with joy.

Many ancient traditions teach that we choose our life purpose and direction prior to incarnating on this earth. The principles of astrology and numerology, for example, are founded on this belief and offer guidance and insight into what that purpose might be. For most of us, however, discovering our life purpose is not so straightforward.

The questions below, which are also included in the Manifest Your Desires workbook in Part Two, will help you discover what really matters to you and what issues you are passionate about. Discovering this passion is the key to discovering your life purpose. I suggest that you find some quiet time when you won't be interrupted to answer the questions below. Taking time to reflect on your answers might reveal the seeds to your passion and purpose.

- If you had more free time, how would you spend it?
- What experiences have moved you to tears of joy?
- What habits of others most annoy you?
- What unresolved world issues (e.g., religious strife, environmental destruction, overpopulation, unethical leadership, etc.) most trouble you?
- How do you want to be remembered?
- If you were independently wealthy, how would you spend your time?
- If you could be famous for 10 minutes, what would you be acknowledged for?
- If you won the lottery tomorrow, how would you spend your $10M, and how would it alter your current life?

From the Buddhist perspective, the way we live our lives today will influence the quality of our lives in the future, both in this lifetime and in future lifetimes. I think it is best to just focus on this lifetime, and if we focus on being present every minute we will become more conscious of how our life unfolds as we intend it to. When you start to develop the seeds of what your life purpose is, you may notice that you are not as much at the effect of events and circumstances surrounding you. Individuals with a clear life purpose are not as vulnerable to the stresses of daily life. When shattering personal or world events occur, they can step back and reflect on how they can contribute to improving the situation. They have developed deeper clarity about what issues they can influence and that are of greatest importance to them, and don't try and take on the problems of their friends, family members, and the world in general.

FIND YOUR LIFE'S WORK

Work is love made visible. And if you cannot work with love
but only with distaste, it is better that you should leave
your work and sit at the gate of the temple and take alms of
those who work with love.

KAHLIL GIBRAN, *The Prophet*

How many people do you know whose work is their passion or qualifies as their "life work"? "Life work" is different from a job or a profession. It is work, tasks, or even activities in which one finds mental, emotional, and spiritual fulfillment. Our lives have greater meaning when our purpose and our work are consistent. When you can bring all of yourself to your work, when you understand how this opportunity is contributing to your personal growth, you fulfill inner yearnings for self-expression and fulfillment regardless of compensation or status. Being energized by your work in this way helps you manifest your dreams into reality. Since the majority of our waking hours are spent doing some type of work, our jobs and careers are a primary vehicle for developing personal power.

Unfortunately, most people end up in their jobs by accident or by necessity. Some, for example, end up working in a big corporation when a smaller entrepreneurial environment would be more fulfilling. Others end up be-hind a desk all day when their passion is being outdoors in nature. Many who begin a job with enthusiasm and commitment get worn down by orga-nizational dysfunction. Very few choose their jobs in the spirit of a life work that's in line with their life purpose.

It's no surprise, then, that many people feel bored, frustrated, or power-less in their jobs. Some studies have shown that as many as 75 percent of working people in the United States are dissatisfied with their job or career. In their bestselling book *Now, Discover Your Strengths*, Marcus Bucking-ham and Donald O. Clifton write that "Globally, only 20 percent of em-ployees working in the large organizations we surveyed feel that their strengths are in play every day. Most bizarre of all, the longer an employee stays with an organization and the higher he climbs the traditional career ladder, the less likely he is to strongly agree that he is playing to his strengths." It's sad to think of so many spending so much time doing work that does not tap into their unique gifts.

FINDING YOUR UNIQUE TALENTS

Thousands of geniuses live and die undiscovered—either by themselves or by others.

MARK TWAIN,
quoted in *The Autobiography of Mark Twain*
by Charles Neider

At a certain stage in life your dream of becoming an astronaut is no longer realistic, but lifework can start anytime. We all come into this life with unique talents and abilities that are always in reach if we seek them out. Ap-plying those natural skills in our work is the core of any lifework, and part of our purpose for being on this planet. Ironically, they are often the ones we do so effortlessly that we simply overlook them.

Buckingham and Clifton provide several examples of what a unique talent might look like to the untrained eye:

Talent is often described as "a special natural ability or aptitude." [It] is any recurring pattern of thought, feeling, or behavior that can be productively applied. Thus, if you are instinctively inquisitive, this is a talent. If you are competitive, this is a talent. If you are charming, this is a talent. If you are persistent, this is a talent. If you are responsible, this is a talent. *Any* recurring pattern of thought, feeling, or behavior is a talent if this pattern can be productively applied.

Think about your own life and work. What are your special talents, qualities, and values? What skills do you receive acknowledgement for from your peers, family, and co-workers? Does your current job situation adequately incorporate those abilities? How about your career objectives and the direction you seem to be heading? All of us want to make a contribution to something greater than just ourselves. Do you see this happening in your workplace or how your future seems to be unfolding?

Here are some additional questions to help you determine whether your current job or career has the qualities of life work:

- Do you love your job or career?
- Do you wake up in the morning eager to seize the day?
- Does your work enable you to live a balanced life?
- Are you contributing your creative talents at work?
- Are you acknowledged for your unique contributions?
- Are you making a difference?
- Is your work helping to make the world a better place?
- Are you clear about the legacy you want to leave?
- Are you creating and committed to something that is bigger than you?

If your current situation falls short of where you want it to be, then consider the following suggestions as a way to change your perspective and begin the process of redirecting your energies toward something of meaning and purpose:

- View your work as an adventure and an opportunity for personal growth.
- Understand that there are no accidents, and that you are working exactly where you're supposed to in order to learn valuable insights about yourself.
- Embrace the fact that you alone are responsible for your actions and for creating your life and reality.

POWER NOTES

- We each possess our own particular genius and the ability to make a distinctive contribution to our relationships, workplaces, and communities.
- When you integrate power, passion, and purpose—the essence of personal mastery—you can accomplish great things.
- When you live your life purpose, you are much less susceptible to fear, anger, guilt, or the need for approval.
- "Lifework" is different from a job or a profession. It describes a job in which one finds mental, emotional, and spiritual fulfillment.
- Our lives have greater meaning when our purpose and our jobs are consistent.
- All of us want to make a contribution to something greater than just ourselves.

STEP 2

INCREASE YOUR INSTINCT AND INTELLIGENCE

CHAPTER THREE

Whole-Body Intelligence

The power of presence means we are able to bring all four intelligences forward: mental, emotional, spiritual, and physical. Some individuals carry such presence that we identify them as charismatic or magnetic personalities. We are drawn to them; they captivate our interest even before they speak or we know anything about them.

ANGELES ARRIEN, PH.D.,
*The Four Fold Way:
Walking the Paths of the
Warrior, Teacher, Healer, and Visionary*

Angeles Arrien, a well-known cultural anthropologist and popular author, has described *presence* as the ability to manage and integrate four kinds of intelligences: mental, emotional, spiritual, and physical. These four intelligences can also be thought of as the four principle areas where we focus our attention and energy. We all have the capacity to improve each area, but those of us who live in Western cultures spend most of our time developing our mental skills.

People with the ability to alter the reality of others purely by their own presence have mastered all four of these intelligences. We notice such individuals the moment they enter a room. They are present; they live in the moment. They have a dynamic inner quality that we often interpret as power. And yet such people don't overpower a room or those they're with;

they actually empower others by reflecting back to them their own inner strengths, allowing them to feel capable, complete, interesting, and worthy. Such people inspire and energize us.

In *A Passion for the Possible: A Guide to Realizing Your True Potential*, Jean Houston writes:

> Many of the so-called larger-than-life people differ from the rest of us chiefly in this respect: It is not that they are actually larger in mind and soul or more brilliant. Rather, they are profoundly present to the stuff of their lives, to what is happening within themselves as well as around them. They use and enjoy their senses more, they inhabit with keen awareness their bodies as well as their minds, they explore the world of imagery and imagination, they rehearse memories, engage in projects that reinvent the world, are serious about life but laugh at themselves, and seek to empower others as they would be empowered. Quite simply, they are cooking on more burners.

Early cultures believed that personal power was based on the development of the same four intelligences, though they may not have described them as such, and that disease could occur if any one of them were blocked or undeveloped. So they created numerous rituals, tests, and practices to help people develop and strengthen them in a balanced way. Most of their methods were based on maintaining the quality and flow of one's energy. Such practices are as valid today as they were centuries ago.

INCREASING WHOLE-BODY INTELLIGENCE

Today it's well accepted that humans are comprised of bodies, minds, emotions, and something called *spirit*, yet we continue to overemphasize the development of our mental abilities. This over-reliance on the rational/analytical shuts us off from our instinct and intuition, which draw their vitality from the other three intelligences and which are essential ingredients in an optimally functioning life. It's not about discounting the mental—your left brain has an important role to play. But choices based solely on that, or for that matter emphasizing any one intelligence over another, will never truly serve us. To access all of your inner wisdom and the healing energy of the universe, you need to go beyond the "lens of linearity" and engage all four of your intelligences. From such a place of balance, you can't help but make wise decisions.

What follows are brief discussions of each intelligence, along with some suggestions to help you enable your "whole-body" experience.

PHYSICAL INTELLIGENCE

"Physical intelligence" is often associated with athletes or those who have mastered such disciplines as yoga or martial arts, but it's really about being at home in your body and learning to listen to the signals it is sending you. Indigenous peoples and "primitive" cultures are quite adept at this—living so close to nature, they rely on their physical "knowing" to respond intelligently to the world around them. Those who are physically attuned:

- Are grounded and present and in their bodies.
- Know and consume the foods that are best for them.
- Know and respect the capacity and limits of their bodies.
- Know when they need rest or downtime.
- Are free of nagging discomforts such as colds, flu, and headaches.
- Avoid injuries.
- Have an ability to self-diagnose their own illnesses and know which remedies would be most appropriate.
- Respect the physical boundaries of others, to know how much "space" to give them.

There is no one right way to develop your physical intelligence, which is good because everyone is different. Through commitment and experimentation, you will find the right routines and practices that work for your particular body and bring you closer toward your goals. In general, any activity that helps you focus on your body—on being in your body—and keep it healthy will contribute to the development of physical intelligence. The suggestions below represent a partial list.

- Exercise at least four times a week; this can include walking, which is recommended over all other forms of activity.
- Avoid or moderate the eating of white sugar, white flour, salt, processed foods such as those found in cans, and factory-farmed meat, replacing with fresh and/or "organic" foods whenever possible.
- Take a high-quality nutritional supplement every day.
- Visit a chiropractor and "indulge" in massage therapy or some other professional bodywork.
- Take frequent time out to breathe slowly and deeply.
- Drink enough water—eight cups a day is recommended.
- Get sufficient rest and sleep.
- Use homeopathy, acupuncture, or acupressure to stimulate energy.
- Move your body in different ways with such practices as yoga, Chi Gung, or Tai Chi. They will slow you down and heighten your physical sensations and awareness.
- Schedule time for inner reflection.

EMOTIONAL INTELLIGENCE

One of the areas that we most neglect to develop is our emotional intelligence. We live in a culture where strong expressions of emotion are discouraged—unless, of course, we're cheering our favorite sports team. To display anger in public is socially unacceptable. And while most of us are comfortable demonstrating love to our children and significant others, we can get uncomfortable expressing warm feelings to people beyond our immediate family.

The more you can get in touch with your unexpressed emotions, the more easily you'll be able to activate your emotional intelligence. This will lead to making better decisions and keeping the flow of energy moving. When your thoughts, emotions, and actions are consistent, you are connected to your wisdom and power. But when you ignore your feelings, when you aren't in touch with your anger, fear, sadness, or even joy, then your perceptions, choices, and actions will be negatively influenced. To make choices from a place of personal power instead of weakness and indecision, we need to reclaim and transform the parts of ourselves that cause us to feel anxious, uncertain, or fearful.

Psychologist Daniel Goleman has been studying human emotions while a professor at Harvard University. His research and beliefs have led him to place a high emphasis on emotion as the center of aptitude for conscious living. He believes that emotional balance can support health, well-being, and everyday functionality in a number of ways. As he writes in his bestselling book, *Emotional Intelligence:*

> Those who are at the mercy of impulse—who lack self-control—suffer a moral deficiency: The ability to control impulse is the base of will and character. By the same token, the root of altruism lies in empathy, the ability to read emotions in others; lacking a sense of another's need or despair, there is no caring. And if there are any two moral stances that our times call for, they are precisely these, self-restraint and compassion.

In the Huna practices of Native Hawaiians, emotions are believed to be movements of energy throughout the body, and that this flow of emotion comes from our thoughts. Thus, in changing the way we think, we change the emotions we're experiencing. The Hawaiians also believe that the expression of love—or the lack of it—characterizes how we feel about ourselves and act toward others, and that to heal is to love and to love is to heal.

No matter what system of study and belief is embraced, most people with healthy emotional intelligence:

- Have a highly developed understanding of themselves, and use that self-awareness to become a better person.
- Are aware of their thoughts, moods, and feelings.
- Have strong self-control over their emotional impulses and are aware of the effects of toxic emotions.
- Have highly developed social skills and are able to harmonize with others.

Listed below are a variety of methods for increasing your emotional intelligence. Some, like color therapy, are more subtle and indirect; others such as psychotherapy will deeply and directly engage you. This is not an exhaustive list, but again, it will give you a sense of the different approaches available, and what might make sense for you.

- *Aromatherapy* is the practice of using the essences of plants to promote the health and well-being of the body, mind, and emotional spirit. The essences, called essential oils, can restore balance and harmony to your body and your life.
- *Color therapy* is based on the belief that the human body is composed of energy fields, and that imbalances of energy indicate an excess or deficiency. Color therapy is a technique of restoring balance by means of applying color to the body or even reflecting on different colors as a means of healing. Color light therapy was used 2,500 years ago by Pythagoras and in ancient Egypt, China, and Tibet.
- *Hypnosis* is the process of entering a deep state of relaxation with the assistance of a hypnotist. It is a trance state characterized by extreme suggestibility, relaxation, and heightened imagination, but the subject being hypnotized is alert the entire time. Hypnosis has helped many individuals discontinue an addictive habit.
- *Laughter* as a form of therapy became more widely known when Norman Cousins published *Anatomy of an Illness* in 1979, which documented how he reversed a painful disease. He found that 15

minutes of hearty laughter could produce two hours of pain-free sleep.

- *Music and sound therapy* is being used to modify ineffective learning patterns, promote emotional growth, and improve social behavior patterns. It has proven effective in treating depression, schizophrenia, autism, anxiety disorders, and post-traumatic stress disorder. Sound therapy was recognized as a method of achieving balance from within in the ancient civilizations of Africa, Egypt, India, and China, and among the Aboriginal tribes and Native Americans.
- *Psychotherapy* is a term used to describe a variety of talking therapies used to treat mild and moderate forms of depression and mental or emotional problems. It involves talking to a licensed professional during a scheduled series of appointments.
- *Therapeutic touch* is a type of energy medicine whereby the therapist moves his or her hands over the patient's energy field, directing the flow of "chi" or "prana" so the patient can heal. Energy healers restore the energy field to a state of balance, bringing harmony to a proper alignment. The restoration of integrity to the patient's energy field makes it possible for the body to heal itself.

MENTAL INTELLIGENCE

Most of us have spent the better part of our lives developing our mental capacities at the expense of our other intelligences, so I won't spend too much time on it. But it's still important to keep our minds versatile and to forge new neural pathways, especially as we grow older. The mind is a powerful tool; keeping it healthy and active is vital to overall health. Some ways to accomplish this include:

- Playing games that stimulate the mind
- Choosing enriching reading material
- Doing challenging crossword puzzles

- Engaging in discussions on thought-provoking topics
- Doing visualizations and affirmations
- Learning a new language

The practice of meditation may be the most important tool in sharpening your mental skills. By helping you stop or at least slow down the incessant movement of your rational mind, you allow other sensations and feelings to float into—and out of—your conscious awareness. Meditation is probably the single most powerful and effective way to improve your mental energy and intelligence by—ironically—giving your brain a rest! Meditation is discussed in more detail in Step 4—Choose Your Ideal Energy Practice, and simple meditation practices are included in Part Two under Energy Practices.

SPIRITUAL INTELLIGENCE

Spiritual intelligence is our human capacity to ask ultimate questions about the meaning of life, and to experience simultaneously the seamless connection between each of us and the world in which we live.

RICHARD N. WOLMAN, PH.D.,
Thinking with Your Soul:
Spiritual Intelligence and Why It Matters

Spirituality is the individual process of discovering the divine within us. Spiritual practice acts as a catalyst for inner change and growth. Spiritual energy is what directs our physical, mental, and emotional energies. Spiritual intelligence is rooted in a worldview that we are connected to a higher power and source of energy, and that this universal intelligence supports us. In fact, our greatest joy comes from a feeling of connection with "all that is."

Marsha Sinetar describes spiritual intelligence as an "illuminated brightness," and says that those with spiritual intelligence are the pathfinders who speak of unfamiliar realities.

"The happiest people that I know," she writes in *The Power of Meditation and Prayer*, "are not necessarily traditionally religious. But they seem to be people who have cultivated a spiritual understanding of themselves and their Creator—whatever term you would put to that. They've settled into their place in the largest scheme of things. Perhaps they've invented it. For one reason or another, they don't really fear what's on the other side. They've come to terms with their transitions. Spiritual maturity brings great harmony."

It's impossible to generalize how those with highly developed spiritual intelligence act on a day-to-day basis, but there are some common characteristics:

- Support their co-workers instead of viewing them as competitors.
- Know when to break from chaos and meditate or sit quietly.
- Connect their work with a sacred purpose.
- Advocate ways that contribute to the well-being of others.
- Place a high degree of importance on personal interactions.
- Feel a strong connection to others in a group and gain meaning from this connection.
- Are concerned with the morality of their actions at work and the ethical conduct of leaders.
- Have a deep relationship with nature.
- Are often interested in the search for greater meaning in life.

Any practice that quiets the mind and opens us up to other sources of knowing can lead to spiritual health and intelligence. This can be a very personal journey, and there are countless ways to go about it. Some that I've relied on include the following; others are discussed in Step 4—Choose Your Ideal Energy Practice.

- Prayer
- Meditation
- Reiki
- Regular time for reflection
- Time spent in nature

Optimal health, balance, and alignment occur when all four areas of "energy intelligence" are aligned and integrated. This alignment will improve your instinct and intuition in order for you to make life choices and decisions faster and more accurately. When all four areas of intelligence are aligned, you will produce results in your life that might once have seemed miraculous. Self-healing and mastery become real, not wishes or fictions.

POWER NOTES

- *Presence* is the ability to manage and integrate four kinds of intelligence: mental, emotional, spiritual, and physical.
- Over-reliance on the rational/analytical shuts us off from our instinct and intuition.
- Physical intelligence is often associated with athletes or those who have mastered such disciplines as yoga or martial arts, but it's really about being at home in your body.
- There is no one right way to develop your physical intelligence, which is good because everyone is different.
- People with healthy emotional intelligence have a highly developed understanding of themselves, and use that self-awareness to become a better person.
- Meditation is probably the single most powerful and effective way to improve your mental energies and intelligence by — ironically — giving your brain a rest!
- Spiritual energy is what directs our physical, mental, and emotional energies.
- Spiritual intelligence is rooted in a worldview that we are connected to a higher power and source of energy, and that this universal intelligence supports us.
- Optimal health occurs when all four areas of "energy intelligence" are aligned and integrated.

CHAPTER FOUR

Improve Your Intuition and Instinct

> The moment of truth, the sudden emergence of a new insight, is an act of intuition. Such intuitions give the appearance of miraculous flashes, or short-circuits of reasoning. In fact they may be likened to an immersed chain, of which only the beginning and the end are visible above the surface of consciousness.
>
> ARTHUR KOESTLER,
> *The Act of Creation*

Intuition is often referred to as "gut instinct," that physical sense we get when we know if a choice is right or wrong or if a person is trustworthy or not. All of us have experienced such knowing—an inspiration, a revealed truth, a moment of brilliance that brought a fresh new sense of creativity to our lives. Such awareness is triggered not by linear thinking but by direct knowing through a nonlinear process.

Peter Senge, a noted management futurist, has said that personal mastery is intuition integrated with reason. The Sufis describe intuition as a direct knowing without the conscious use of learning. This creative, intuitive process requires a state of consciousness that is very different from our everyday awareness.

Those who can readily access this source of inner perception have highly attuned whole-body intelligence. They are able to receive and process information from a variety of sources and at a variety of levels, e.g., not just through sight or sound but through absorbing textures and patterns. By accessing this larger "field" of information and acting on what they learn, they make better choices about their personal and professional lives. Those without this ability end up drawing from a much narrower band of "data" when making such decisions, and are thus more vulnerable to less-than-optimal choices.

DEVELOPING YOUR INTUITIVE SKILLS

We've all had *psychic experiences* in our lives. These can manifest as the inexplicable feeling we get when we visit a place for the first time and know we've been there before, or when we're engaged in conversation and suddenly feel as if we've already had this same conversation with this same individual. That's right—a déjà vu experience is a psychic event!

When the telephone rings, do you sometimes know who it is before picking up the phone? Have you ever been in a situation where you suddenly felt you were in danger and decided to take another path? Have you sensed that something was wrong with a relative or friend and called to check up on them—and discovered you were right? How about some of the following:

- Can you tell if someone is lying?
- Do you make decisions easily?
- Do you sense things before they happen?
- Do you revise your plans if you get a bad feeling?
- Do you see solutions to problems easily?
- Do you trust yourself to make decisions?
- Are there lots of coincidences in your life?

If you answered yes to five or more of the previous questions, you have highly developed intuitive skills. These experiences happen to all of us, and more frequently when we accept them as a natural part of life, and more frequently still when all of our intelligences are activated. The Hindu, Tibetan, and Egyptian cultures refer to the "third eye"—located behind the pineal gland in the center of the forehead—as the center of psychic awareness. Individuals with highly developed third-eye vision have the capacity to see and predict events in the future. For me it's like having a small computer monitor in my head that I can scroll forward to the future or backward to the past. The ability to see into the future is sometimes called "second sight." And despite what you may believe, most self-proclaimed psychics are no better at predicting the future than "ordinary" people like you and me. We all have different types and degrees of psychic abilities, depending on the extent to which we've trusted and developed them. Self-trust plays an important part in intuition.

The first step in developing and refining these intuitive skills is learning the art of observation. In an environment of acceleration and change, it becomes ever more important to "pause and consider" even as it becomes more difficult to do so. And yet the demands of each day, with our commitments to career, family, friends, and community, often leave little room for reflection. The result is people pursuing objectives that are inappropriate to their true needs or unlikely to happen, and precious time and energy are wasted. When we tell ourselves "There's no *time* for reflection," we're forgetting to consider the time and money that may be wasted by acting before we've observed and reflected.

Making time for contemplation leads to new realizations and important discoveries that can easily slip through the cracks of our busyness. When we slow down and take a step back, the next appropriate action becomes more apparent. One of the keys to establishing power and control over your life is to spend part of each day alone and to use that time to reflect on your current feelings and challenges.

Developing such a practice is additionally important because one of the ways we receive information is through our subconscious minds. Our minds work like computers, processing thousands of bits of data every day.

Some of it we're aware of, but much passes through unnoticed. In our hyperactive, fast-paced lives we prevent ourselves from tapping into that subconscious stream, which contains knowledge and impressions that might be very valuable, for example, a subtle connection between two seemingly unrelated events that sheds new light on a situation.

KNOWING IN AN INSTANT

In our fast-paced world, we need to learn how to make decisions in an instant. The effectiveness and accuracy of your decisions is not related to how much time you spend thinking about your options. The process of gathering opinions and as much information as possible, then analyzing and deliberating over your choices and options, will not necessarily support you in making better life decisions. In high-stake situations, there is no time to review your options. You need to learn how to listen to your own inner wisdom and develop more fully your instinct and whole-body intelligence.

A story that illustrates the value of having a highly developed instinct and knowing the right decision in an instant was demonstrated by the Moken, an indigenous and ancient tribe who live off the coast of Thailand and Burma. In December 2004, before the enormous tsunami came crashing down on seaside villages in Southeast Asia, the water receded, the dolphins swam for deeper water, and the elephants stampeded towards higher ground. The Moken recognized that the water receding wasn't ordinary and rushed to the hills; there were no casualties in their village.

The Moken who were fishing off the coast of Burma headed for the safety of deeper water, but the Burmese fisherman did not. A Moken elder stated "they saw nothing, they looked at nothing, they don't know how to look." These are the skills we need to develop to operate more effectively in our modern world. We need to know, in an instant, what is the best option. We need to learn how to look at patterns and nuances in order to make decisions instinctively.

BECOMING MORE GROUNDED

As I discussed in the previous chapter, developing and balancing our four intelligences provides us with a number of important benefits. One of them is that we become more *grounded*. Being grounded means learning how to be present—not regretting what we did yesterday or even an hour ago, or worrying about what we're going to do tomorrow, but simply paying attention to what is happening in the moment. It requires that we are aware of and comfortable in our physical bodies, and able to stay there when the distractions around us—rude people, impending deadlines, worries over money—conspire to pull us toward anxiety or escape. It's difficult, if not impossible, to create anything new until we've learned to stay in the present moment. Remember that overused maxim "Be here now"? Well, it may be a cliché, but its message is right on.

For Angeles Arrien, the key to intuition is the ability to stay focused and present. As she wrote in a 1997 article for *Intuition* magazine:

> I try to get people to listen fully, to be here with their whole heart.
> If you are able to do that, you see what people are really doing with
> their lives, what their intentions are, what kind of feedback and
> encouragement they need. You're able to be so much more effective
> in your work and personal relationships because you're paying
> attention. You can call the special knowledge that comes from this
> ESP or intuition, but its root is still presence. When we learn to
> be fully present, we are much more in touch with our non rational
> ways of perceiving.

Unfortunately, the entire force of our culture either pulls us away from the present moment or stuffs too much information into it. The emphasis is on doing and moving, never staying still, bouncing from one distraction to another. Our fast-paced lifestyle causes us to move too fast and so lose our focus on the present. Anything that takes us out of the body and out of our self-awareness takes us farther away from our instincts and intuition. When we aren't in the present, we can't connect intelligently with our immediate reality. We lose touch with our unique gifts. This lack of a present-moment focus afflicts everyone regardless of title, prestige, or influence. Conditioned by our culture, responding constantly to a barrage of stimuli, staying present seems an unattainable task, yet one that must be mastered to access our innate gifts.

POWER NOTES

- Intuition is often referred to as "gut instinct," that physical sense we get when we know if a choice is right or wrong, or if a person is trustworthy or not.
- Anything that takes us out of the body and out of our self-awareness takes us farther away from our instincts and intuition.
- It's difficult, if not impossible, to create anything new until we've learned to stay in the present moment.
- We all have different types and degrees of psychic abilities, depending on the extent to which we've trusted and developed them.
- The first step in developing and refining these intuitive skills is learning the art of observation.
- When we slow down and take a step back, the next appropriate action becomes more apparent.
- One of the keys to establishing power and control over your life is to spend part of each day alone, and to use that time to reflect on your current feelings and challenges.

LEARN AND APPLY THE PRINCIPLES OF ENERGY MANAGEMENT

CHAPTER FIVE

Energy and Transformation

There are fundamental truths on which our "understanding"
of the universe is founded. These truths are not dependent
on science, religion, or any other thought pattern; they just are!
One of these truths is that everything in the universe is an
expression of energy or, put another way, nothing that exists
is devoid of energy.

ANDY BAGGOTT with DR. ANDREW TRESSIDER,
The Encyclopedia of Energy Healing

This book is about transformation: yours, and the world you live
in. It happens when you think of your life in terms of energy and
how that energy works. As you master the movement of this energy, you start to master yourself.

Every day, at some level, you shift your energy to meet the demands of
your responsibilities, commitments, and circumstances. Whether it's spending
time as a parent or being productive at work, you are constantly making
internal adjustments, depending on the situation. When traumatic, personal,
or world events challenge your belief in God or humanity, you shift your
perspective at an even deeper level to cope and move forward.

This ability to adapt to change, to alter your behavior with a wide variety of people and situations, is "power in action." Not a "power over" that
seeks to manipulate others, but the power to create circumstances that can
benefit your own life, a power that comes from inner strength and clarity, a

power that reflects your ability to access and redirect your personal energy. Power and energy properly aligned will help you make and follow through on decisions that will improve your life at every level: personally, financially, in your relationships, and ultimately in the world around you.

THE FIVE PRINCIPLES OF ENERGY MANAGEMENT

All energy practices, from meditation, toning, and chanting to Chi Gung and yoga, support the development of personal power by helping you focus your attention on the skills of sensing, feeling, and knowing rather than thinking, analyzing, and speculating. These "right brain" abilities are the key to accessing your inner wisdom, consciously working with energy, and transforming uncomfortable realities such as a troubled relationship or a difficult work situation. In fact, "managing your energy"—not just figuratively but literally—has become a foundational element of wise decision-making. As noted by Jim Loehr and Tony Schwartz in their book *The Power of Full Engagement*,

> Performance, health and happiness are grounded in the skillful management of energy. The number of hours in a day is fixed, but the quantity and quality of energy available to us is not. It is our most precious resource. The more we take responsibility for the energy we bring to the world, the more empowered and productive we become. The more we blame others or external circumstances, the more negative and compromised our energy is likely to be.

And so, in the same way that managing your time, your day, or your finances requires a certain understanding of how those things work, managing your energy requires a level of awareness of what energy is and how it works, which involves paying attention to what your thoughts and your body is telling you and then taking appropriate actions. It's about learning a new language—the language of "energy management." Following are five guiding principles:

1. Everything in the Universe Is Energy

According to the latest findings of quantum physics, all physical, visible, tangible, and animate objects—whether human, animal, plant, mineral, or man-made materials and structures—are comprised of differing energy densities. All invisible and inanimate objects and qualities—thoughts, emotions, feelings and dreams, and even our spirits—are also comprised of different energy densities. Each density also has its own system of energy within it; the more complex the organism, the more complex the system.

2. The Quality of Your Life Reflects the State of Your Physical, Emotional, Mental, and Spiritual Energy.

Human beings are the most complex species on the planet, comprised of various energy centers (see Chapter Six for more information) that are related to physical, emotional, mental, and spiritual health. When you learn to manage these fundamental components of who you are and identify/self-diagnose the source of a misalignment at whatever level it occurs, you will increase your vitality and maximize your ability to make effective personal and professional decisions.

3. Events and Circumstances Will Inevitably Force You Out of Alignment and Off Balance.

Energy reacts to its environment: to your thoughts, feelings, and beliefs, to the food you eat and the quality of your physical surroundings, and to the pressures of daily life. When these influences are healthy and life-supporting, your system runs smoothly and your life is experienced as "working." When those influences are unhealthy, they will have negative impacts on your equilibrium, turning joy into sadness and hope into despair, and challenging you at every turn.

4. All Expressions of Energy Will Alter Their State, Composition, and Density Instantaneously.

Think of the effect that fire has on such elements as water when it's boiled or wood when it's burned. The change of state is almost immediate (e.g., from tree trunk to ash and air). In the same way, consider how lethargy, sadness, or depression can be reduced and even eliminated when you think of someone you love or listen to uplifting music or talk to someone who makes you laugh or take a walk in nature. Immediately you feel lighter or more energized. Everyone has the skill to alter their energy, their internal reality, in such ways.

5. Disciplines are Available for Reestablishing Physical, Emotional, Mental, and Spiritual Alignment.

For thousands of years, people have followed disciplines that enabled them to heal physical ailments, counteract disease, and return to a state of inner and outer balance. The practices of breath work, movement, sound, and stillness are designed to rebalance and re-energize body, mind, and spirit.

ENERGY PRACTICE AS PART OF DAILY LIFE

The principles of energy were founded on the idea that "life force" energy, both in animate and inanimate forms, emanates from God, the Great Spirit, the "One"—some kind of ultimate source. The spiritual disciplines, healing practices, and personal growth and development systems associated with those principles are designed to help one align with this life force. Some of the more common include meditation, prayer, *Huna*, Kabalah, visualization, yoga, Chi Gung, Tai Chi, Tibetan Rites, singing, chanting, toning, dancing, feng shui, and Ayurveda. The variations are endless, but all of them seek to restore and maintain optimal levels of physical, mental, spiritual, and emotional energy.

In ancient times, these principles, disciplines, and practices were often incorporated into every aspect of daily living—work responsibilities, healthcare, relationships and family dynamics, even celebrations and contemplation. There were no specific times or days that a person prayed or expressed gratitude; such devotion and practice was intricately woven into every thought and action. The ancients viewed them as necessary for keeping their bodies, minds, and spirits functioning fully and effectively. Just as we know that our bodies need food and water and our cars need gasoline, the ancients knew they needed energy practices for healthy living.

Such deep integration of life force energy beliefs and daily practice is not characteristic of life in the West. The acuity of three of the four intelligences—emotional, physical, and spiritual—that have guided humans for millennia has become weakened over time by our over-reliance on mental intelligence. The situation is akin to operating on one cylinder instead of four. We may have gotten away with this in the past, but the increasing complexity of today's world demands a more full-ranged response.

Fortunately, we live in a time when it has never been easier to initiate change or nurture creative ideas into existence. We have the power to alter our actions, our beliefs, and our lives *instantaneously* and for the better; we have merely forgotten that we possess these skills. They are part of our heritage, part of our DNA. And so as indigenous and shamanic cultures mastered the ability to operate on all four levels, so can we. In the chapters that follow, you will learn more about how these energies and intelligences work, and how to incorporate them into your busy schedule.

And more and more people are doing just that, changing their lives and the world around them. Interest in vibrational medicine, energy diagnostic systems, and energy-enhancing exercises is rising dramatically. Mainstream Americans in growing numbers are applying the disciplines of ancient traditions to produce practical and immediate results in their lives. From yoga and meditation to Chi Gung and chanting, these timeless technologies are enabling individuals to reduce stress, feel more energized, make life decisions with greater ease and confidence, increase their creativity and productivity, and improve their overall health and well-being.

POWER NOTES

- All energy practices help you to realize your "personal power" by focusing your attention on the skills of sensing, feeling, and knowing rather than thinking, analyzing, and speculating.
- Managing your energy has become a foundational element of good health and consists of five principles of energy management.

  Principle One: Everything in the universe is energy.

  Principle Two: The quality of your life reflects the state of your physical, emotional, mental, and spiritual energy.

  Principle Three: Events and circumstances will inevitably force you out of alignment and off balance.

  Principle Four: All expressions of energy will alter their state, composition, and density instantaneously.

  Principle Five: Disciplines are available for reestablishing physical, emotional, mental, and spiritual alignment.

- Daily application of the principles of energy and integration of the four intelligences will change your life.

CHAPTER SIX

Managing Your Energy

> Researchers will discover that the etheric body is an energetic
> growth template that guides the growth and development as
> well as the dysfunction and demise of all human beings. Based
> upon the evolved insights of these enlightened researchers,
> medicine will begin to comprehend that it is at the etheric
> level that many diseases have their origins.
>
> RICHARD GERBER,
> *Vibrational Medicine:*
> *New Choices for Healing Ourselves*

All ancient cultures were founded on the knowledge that everything in the universe is energy. The elements of air, water, fire, and earth are all made up of energy, each with differing densities. Animals, plants, and even buildings are composed of energy with diverse qualities and densities. They also believed that human beings were bundles of energy—complex and subtle networks of energy fields that, in modern terms, interfaced with our physical and cellular systems. They referred to this "energy body" as the *etheric* body or the *aura*—an energetic blueprint of the physical body. When the energetic body is perfectly aligned with the physical body, great reservoirs of creativity and wisdom become available. When it isn't, pathological breakdowns can occur, manifesting physically, emotionally, mentally, or spiritually. Fortunately, this ancient wisdom still exists today in cultures throughout the world.

CH'I, PRANA, AND MANA

Although the concept of an energy system has been relatively unknown in Western philosophy, it is fundamental to the philosophies of the East. The Chinese refer to this system as *chi* (also ch'i or qi), while it's called *prana* in ancient Hindu texts.

Chi or prana represents the life force of all animate things. The origins of the concept of chi can be traced to several ancient religions and belief systems, most notably documented in the writings of the Taoist philosophers Lao Tse, Chuang Tse, and Confucius.

The health practices of Chi Gung, acupuncture, and meditation are based on the concept of chi. Ancient schools of healing view acupuncture *meridians* (think of electrical circuits that run just below the surface of the skin) as the foundation of the human anatomy. The Chinese believe that chi enters the body through these meridians, which then act as connectors between acupuncture points and the body's organs.

The Hawaiians refer to energy and lifeforce as *mana*, whose source is the higher self, which they call *aka* or the etheric body. They also believe in chakras and the acupuncture points of Chinese medicine. Hawaiian healers or *kahunas*—men and women—believe that the existence of this etheric pattern enables healing to take place in the body. As the etheric pattern is identical to that of the physical body and always remains whole and intact, it provides the pattern that the physical body can replicate when healing itself.

Native American shamans have practiced energy medicine for more than five thousand years, informed in part by stories handed down from grandmothers to granddaughters that speak of when the Earth was young. Some medicine people believe their spiritual lineage extends even further back. In *The Book of the Hopi*, Frank Waters recounts the Hopi Indians' first revelation—part of their creation myth—that human beings are comprised of complex networks of energy fields that interface with the physical and cellular systems:

The living body of man and the living body of the earth were constructed in the same way. Through each ran an axis, man's axis being the backbone, the vertebral column, which controlled the equilibrium of his movements and his functions. Along this axis were several vibratory centers that echoed the primordial sound of life throughout the universe or sounded a warning if anything went wrong.

ENERGY POLARITY

From Chinese philosophy also comes the concept of "energy polarity." Yang energy is the masculine principle, and represents the creative, generative, and active forces of life. Yin energy is the feminine principle, and represents the passive, receptive, inward aspects of life. Yang is often associated with the image of the sun and light, yin with the moon and darkness. Yang is referred to as ruling the outside of the body, while yin is said to rule the inside. I like to think of them as the dynamic male energy and the magnetic female energy. The basic principle of the practice of Chi Gung, for example, is to unite these two energies. Maintaining a perfect balance of yang and yin energy results in harmony of body, mind, and spirit.

In a world as complex and frantic as ours, however, achieving such a balance has not been easy. Men and now women have been trained to rely on the more dynamic yang approach—charging forward in an aggressive or assertive manner—to deal with problems or search for solutions at the expense of the more receptive and reflective yin. The result may be short term gains or the appearance of career success, but it usually comes at a cost. The following story is typical of such conditioning:

Monica's Story

Monica was director of marketing for a professional services firm. When she started training with me, she complained of how hard she worked at bringing in new business but that her efforts were often futile and she always felt exhausted at the end of the day. Monica had been following a typically yang marketing style, which aggressively focuses on sending out lots of letters and information, lining up as many presentation meetings as you can, and attending numerous regional and national conferences. One of the first things we did was to look at her business plan, which was long on yang—action and outreach—and short on yin, which emphasizes commitments, goals, and intentions (e.g., the number of new clients desired, the types of businesses they were in, the qualities she wanted those clients to possess, and so on). In shifting from a dynamic yang emphasis to a more receptive yin-like approach, Monica needed to learn specific tools for manifesting what she wanted and attracting new opportunities. We also worked on identifying the activities that were taking the most time and achieving the smallest rewards, and which ones were draining her of energy. Monica's new plan achieved a balance of yin and yang, leading to improved results and more vitality at the end of the day.

CHAKRAS: WHEELS OF ENERGY AND LIGHT

Indian yogic texts refer to the subtle energy centers that exist within our bodies as chakras or wheels. These energy hubs are said to resemble whirling vortices, similar to the spiral images of a hurricane as seen from overhead. The spinning of these chakras generates the electromagnetic energy fields of the body. According to this ancient wisdom, there are seven major energy centers in the body, each with a specific function and associated with a major endocrine gland and nerve center— even a color and a musical note.

The following table identifies the seven major chakras, where they are located, and the glands and organs associated with them, as well as their overall function.

Individuals in the West often have strongly developed lower chakras— primarily the first three. Because we have grown up in a culture that isn't comfortable expressing feelings of love and compassion, most Westerners

The Chakras

Chakra	Location	Color	Glands/ Organs	Functions	Musical Note
1st Root *or* Base	Base of the spine	Red	Adrenals/ Kidneys, Colon	Life-force, vitality, instincts, survival	C
2nd Sacral Plexus *or* Navel	Lower abdomen	Orange	Lymphatic/ Bladder, Spleen, Genitals	Procreation, physical force, sexuality	D
3rd Solar Plexus	Between the navel and chest	Yellow	Pancreas/ Stomach, Gallbladder, Liver	Digestion, metabolism, nervous system, emotions	E
4th Heart	Center of the chest	Green	Heart/Lungs, Thymus	Energy, life force, blood circulation	F
5th Throat	Throat area	Sky Blue	Thyroid/ Throat, Hypothalamus	Speech, sound, communication	G
6th Brow (Third Eye)	Between the eyebrows	Indigo (Dark Blue)	Pineal/ Eyes, Ears, Nose	Vision, lower brain (cerebellum), central nervous system	A
7th Crown	Top of the head	Violet	Pituitary/ Central Nervous System	Upper brain (cerebrum)	B

also have a weak fourth or heart chakra. Perhaps it's no coincidence that heart disease is the single leading cause of death in America, according to the American Heart Association. The fifth chakra, known as the throat chakra, is how we communicate our own personal truths. The sixth chakra, represented by the "third eye," is where we get information about the future. It is the psychic/intuitive center of the system. The seventh chakra is the seat of inspiration and connection with divine wisdom. The fourth chakra acts as a bridge between the upper and lower three. If the heart is closed down or undeveloped, it will be difficult to access the information available in the upper chakras and almost impossible to integrate and use the knowledge from both our upper and lower energy centers.

The following table identifies the feelings and attitudes experienced when the chakras are in or out of balance.

Characteristics and Qualities of Chakras

Chakra	In Balance	Out of Balance
1st	Being grounded, vital, healthy, successful,	Insecure, angry, greedy, tense, constipated
2nd	Giving, tolerant, open to receiving, sexual pleasure, open to change	Over-indulgence, confusion, purposelessness, jealousy, envy, impotence
3rd	Personal power, will, mastery, self-control, humor, and laughter	Overwhelmed, self-centered, digestive problems
4th	Compassion, forgiveness, balance, openness, contentment	Repressed, emotional instability, heart and circulation problems
5th	Creative expression, truthful, reliable, wise, kind	Communication and speech problems, ignorance, lack of discernment, depression
6th	Intuition, insight, clairvoyance, concentration, perceptive	Lack of concentration, fear, cynicism, eye problems, headaches
7th	Spiritual will, inspiration, divine wisdom, selfless service	Confusion, lack of inspiration, alienation, senility, depression

When you view yourself from the perspective that your body is essentially made up of energy, you can see the impacts that light, sound, food, chemicals, and the energy of other people can have on you. Vibrational practices based on knowledge of the chakras can assist in altering the frequencies of these energy fields, help sustain a balanced energetic system, and keep body and mind alert and healthy. Although most individuals have little cognitive awareness of how these energies work, it becomes increasingly clear over time (to those who study this system) that the seven chakras are who and what we are—what we feel, how we think, how we express ourselves, how we create, and how we change. In short, the means through which we experience life, perceive reality, and relate to self, others, and the world.

One way to better understand the characteristics and qualities of chakras is to first determine how in or out of balance you believe you are and then look at the correlating boxes in the charts above. Consider the following questions as a place to begin your self-evaluation:

1. Are you feeling insecure?
2. Are you overindulging in food, drugs, alcohol, or socializing?
3. Are you feeling overwhelmed?
4. Are you feeling overemotional?
5. Are you depressed?
6. Do you have difficulty concentrating?
7. Are you feeling uninspired?

All of these challenges may stem from an energy imbalance in one or more of your body's chakras. By answering the following questions, you will shift your state from one of energetic imbalance to a healthier and fully energized state:

1. What steps can I take to become more grounded and to feel healthier?
2. How can I implement activities that I truly enjoy into my daily schedule?

3. Who are the individuals who cause me to lighten up and how can I spend more time with them?

4. What do I need to forgive myself for, and what actions do I need to take to feel more at peace with myself?

5. What do I need to communicate, and to whom, that I have been unwilling to do?

6. What insights do I have about the way I'm living my life that are not part of my truth, and what actions do I need to take to change?

7. What are the sources of inspiration in my life, and what is the contribution I can make that will make a difference in the lives of others?

Another way to become familiar with this particular model of energy is to try to match your observations of friends and family members with corresponding areas on the charts. It's always easier to observe the characteristics of others than to self-diagnose yourself. You can also try using the chart to guess the strengths and weaknesses of well-known people: truth-challenged CEO's with overdeveloped third or underdeveloped fifth chakras; visionary world leaders with strong fourth and seventh charkas, who are in touch with something greater than themselves. Whatever system of energy you feel most drawn to, use it to anchor your understanding of how energy works and how you can use that knowledge to improve your life and contribute to the world around you.

POWER NOTES

- Ancient cultures were founded on the knowledge that everything in the universe is energy.
- When the energetic body is perfectly aligned with the physical body, great reservoirs of creativity and wisdom become available.
- As the etheric pattern is identical to that of the physical body and always remains whole and intact, it provides the pattern that the physical body can replicate when healing itself.
- According to this ancient wisdom, there are seven major energy centers in the body, each with a specific function and associated with a major endocrine gland and nerve center—even a color and a musical note.
- Vibrational practices based on knowledge of the chakras can assist in altering the frequency of these energy fields, help sustain a balanced energetic system, and keep body and mind alert and healthy.
- Whatever system of energy you feel most drawn to, use it to anchor your understanding of how energy works and how you can use that knowledge to improve your life and contribute to the world around you.

CHOOSE YOUR
IDEAL ENERGY PRACTICE

CHAPTER SEVEN

Energy Practices

One reason why the practices of energy healing have been kept so closely guarded is that they are often mistaken for a set of techniques, in the same way that Western medicine is sometimes regarded as a set of procedures. We mistakenly think that we can master energy healing by learning the rules. However, for the shaman it is not about the rules or ideas. It's about vision and Spirit. And while the healing practices often vary from village to village, the Spirit never varies. True healing is nothing less than an awakening to a vision of our healed nature and the experience of infinity.

ALBERTO VILLOLDO, PH.D.,

Shaman, Healer, Sage:

How to Heal Yourself and Others with the

Energy Medicine of the Americas

The term "holistic health" derives from the word *holism,* and refers to the idea discussed in a previous chapter that the physical, mental, emotional, and spiritual aspects of health are interrelated. Instead of treating symptoms or diseases as separate entities to be controlled by drugs or surgery, ancient and "alternative" healing therapies see the human organism as a single interconnected system that facilitates wellness by addressing the total person. Alternative healing therapies are designed to help people help themselves by giving them a deeper understanding of their particular problem and directions for dealing with life in more effective ways.

Homeopathy, for example, enables the immune system to return to optimum levels of functioning. Acupuncture supports the body's ability to regain its structural integrity after it has been impaired. In this philosophical approach, recovery is ultimately an individual's responsibility, aided of course by the particular therapy and with the practitioner providing support as needed.

In this book I'm referring not so much to recovery from a specific trauma (though no less important) but to returning to a state of high-level energy health using practices based primarily on managing the flow of energy.

In the West, this is not generally what we think of when we talk about exercise and health. Most of our physical exercise is aerobic, which uses up oxygen and can be energy depleting. While many energy practices do have a physical component to them, they are primarily anaerobic in nature—they don't use up oxygen, even as they increase and harmonize our energy.

It's true that aerobic exercise such as running, cycling, swimming, walking uphill, and some forms of dancing are great for building overall fitness, and that going to the gym and using weights is excellent for increasing strength and muscle tone. But these activities can actually deplete us of energy or chi if they leave us tired and out of breath. To attain optimal health, aerobic practices need to be balanced with some form of energy exercise.

Research in neurophysiology has shown that an information biofeedback process exists between the brain, the muscles, and the senses. Overextending one's muscular/aerobic efforts inhibits the brain's ability to work with the body. The energy practices of meditation, deep breathing, yoga, Chi Gung, and toning, by comparison, support the exchange of information between the body and the mind and thus create a freer flow of energy.

Matthew's Story

Just out of high school, I began to experience severe low back pain. I'm sure there were psychological reasons attached to my discomfort (the craziness of adolescence, needing to choose a college, and so on), but all I knew was a dull, relentless ache at the base of my spine. I started to do some simple stretching, and then "discovered" yoga. For the next six months I did my daily stretch/yoga routines, and gradually the pain disappeared. It was the beginning of "body consciousness" for me, and a confidence that I actually had some control over my well-being.

A few years ago, I developed problems in my right hip. I again thought of yoga as a treatment, but was afraid that the different postures would increase rather than decrease my discomfort. Nothing else was working though, and I decided to take a six-week yoga course with a local teacher. Tentative at first, pushing gently into the different moves and positions, I found after a couple of weeks that my body was responding positively to the exercises. A few weeks later, none of the movements or positions caused pain in my hip. By the time the class was over, I had regained nearly all of my natural movement and the pain was largely gone. The precision of the yoga postures and the wisdom behind them had once again energized the healing centers of my body.

DIFFERENTIATING DISCIPLINES

The best way to differentiate the various energy practices is to divide them into active/participatory and passive/diagnostic, even though the focus of each is basically the same. Whether you practice yoga or Chi Gung (active/participatory) or receive a Reiki, shiatsu, or acupuncture treatment (passive/diagnostic), the objective is to alter one's energy frequency in order to achieve a greater degree of harmony and wellness. Alternating both approaches is an ideal way to enable the body to achieve optimal realignment. The key unifying belief is that our bodies have the capacity for self-healing.

Such a belief was first proposed by the Greek physician Hippocrates, who concluded that it was necessary to keep all aspects of one's body chemistry in balance. Pythagoras, born more than a century before Hippocrates in 580 B.C., believed that healing came from the spark of life that was within every living being. In 380 B.C., Plato wrote that physicians erred when they separated the soul from the body in providing healing and cures.

A GLOSSARY OF MODERN AND ANCIENT ENERGY-BASED PRACTICES

Chi Gung: Chi Gung works with the "energy of life." The Chinese have long believed in its effectiveness in healing and preventing disease. The practice, generally consisting of a series of bending, stretching, pushing, pulling, and rotating exercises, will increase stamina, balance, coordination, and strength.

Chiropractic: Chiropractors form the second largest group of primary-care providers (after M.D.s) in the United States, and the practice is said to originate with Hippocrates. Most individuals visit a chiropractor to obtain relief from back and neck pain. The adjustments, which vary from gentle to more vigorous, support the realignment of the skeletal structure.

Craniosacral Therapy: This type of therapy initially involved treatment on the cranial (head) and sacral (lower back) areas of the body. The practice is now performed on the entire body, but requires that therapists learn acute listening skills that enable them to perceive the subtle motions of the body. It is particularly beneficial in treating head-related injuries and problems and behavioral disorders in children.

Deep Breathing: Deep, controlled breathing is a natural tranquilizer and rejuvenator. When we breathe deeply, we raise our level of energy, which slows the aging process and enables us to look and feel younger and more vital.

Deep Tissue Therapy: This is a form of deep muscle massage that focuses on the manipulation of connective muscle tissue. Many forms of therapy are included in this category, the most well-known of which is called Rolfing. It is primarily a postural/structural therapy (e.g., straighter spine), but it can also relieve back and neck pain as well as digestive problems.

Kinesiology: This is a form of diagnosis and therapy that uses "muscle testing" to provide information about a patient's flow of energy. It was discovered by a chiropractor, Dr. George Goodheart, who noticed that tight muscles on one side of a body were usually caused by weak muscles on the other side. Utilizing a series of muscle reaction checks, the practitioner searches for weak or strong responses, which then lead to simple but effective treatments.

Massage Therapy: Perhaps the most popular form of "alternative" therapy in the West, massage has been around since at least 15,000 B.C. The most commonly used massage therapy in the West is known as Swedish massage, which was created by a Swedish athlete, Peter Heinrik Link, in the 19th century. The benefits of receiving regular (or even infrequent!) massage most often include muscle relaxation, increased circulation, and pain reduction, but recipients can also experience relief from such chronic conditions as arthritis, fibromyalgia, muscle spasms, and tension headaches. While a massage can improve muscle tone or stimulate weak or inactive muscles, it does not increase muscle strength.

Meditation: The numerous forms of meditation include a focus on breathing, on silent words and phrases, or on particular energy centers of the body. The practice of meditation enables a relaxed state of awareness, insight into problems, a lessening of stress, improved health maintenance, and increased productivity.

Prayer: The process of praying most typically involves making reverent petitions or requests to a deity or higher source. Feng shui can be a form of prayer, as can walking a labyrinth. Affirmations are another form of prayer, as are the prayer wheels used by Tibetan Buddhists. The process of praying sets into motion our deepest desires and opens the door to positive future outcomes.

Reiki: The practice of Reiki (pronounced "ray-key"), as well as Therapeutic Touch and Polarity Therapy, is based on the laying of hands onto specific areas of the body, enabling the clearing of energy blockages. This practice has proven effective in improving circulation, reducing stress levels, and speeding the healing process.

Sacred Dance: Sacred dance has long been an integral part of religious ritual and ceremonial expression, not just an exercise or spectacle. It has been said that dance is the highest expression of humanity's search for spirituality and communion with the divine.

Shiatsu: Shiatsu, which in Japanese means "pressure with fingers," has been practiced as a specific discipline for more than a century (although the concept of acupressure, which is integral to shiatsu, has been around for 5000 years). Shiatsu focuses on a series of specific points along the body's energy meridians and is effective in relieving muscle and joint pain, headaches, and migraines, stimulating circulation and the immune system and raising energy levels.

Tai Chi: Originally developed in China as a martial art, Tai Chi uses slow, smooth body movements to achieve physical and mental relaxation while also strengthening the cardiovascular system. The five essential qualities of Tai Chi are slowness, lightness, balance, calmness, and clarity.

Toning and Sound: The use of sound to improve health and alter awareness has been practiced for thousands of years in many religious traditions. Singing, toning, and chanting have been seen to affect the emotional circuitry of the brain, inducing profound states of relaxation and even improving our learning abilities.

Yoga: Yoga is an Indian science of physical and mental health that is more than 5000 years old. The word "yoga" means "union," and connotes the practice of postures, breath work, and (more commonly in India) meditation to increase strength, flexibility, and a sense of balance.

CHOOSING THE RIGHT THERAPY

There are many disciplines that can access your higher levels of vitality and creativity and enable you to live in greater harmony and balance. It's important to find the ones that most fit your lifestyle and personality, and then to create an approach that is uniquely yours. For example, I've studied the basics of Tai Chi with more than half a dozen teachers. When I follow someone else's discipline, I usually get caught up in doing it their way—precisely and perfectly. In my own practice, however, I just move and allow the energy to move through me. Sometimes my practice resembles Tai Chi and sometimes it resembles an ancient Middle Eastern dance. Although we shouldn't become sloppy in our applications, especially in the beginning, I believe there is always room for improvisation if that feels right to your unique body.

Self-healing and personal change need not be difficult or complex; it only takes a commitment to integrate energy practice into your daily routines. A good place to start is to seek out alternative health clinics that offer a wide range of treatments and therapies. Many of the practices noted above also have governing bodies and professional registries; contact them for advice and information. Medical doctors have become more proactive in recent years in supporting "complementary" therapies, and have their own group of pre-qualified practitioners for patient referral.

Ask friends and health professionals you may already know about their knowledge of such therapies and if they can recommend anyone. Research of any kind is always a good idea. As these therapies move into the mainstream, it's important that you become more educated about their differences in order to make more intelligent choices in managing your own healthcare. I've presented a sampling of such approaches, titled "Energy Practices," in Part Two of this book. The exercises are easy to do and will help you begin your journey.

POWER NOTES

- Alternative healing therapies are designed to help people help themselves by giving them a deeper understanding of their particular problem and directions for dealing with life in more effective ways.
- The energy practices of meditation, deep breathing, yoga, Chi Gung, and toning support the exchange of information between the body and the mind, and thus create a freer flow of energy.
- Whether you practice yoga or Chi Gung (active/participatory), or receive a Reiki, shiatsu, or acupuncture treatment (passive/diagnostic), the objective is to alter one's energy frequency in order to achieve a greater degree of harmony and wellness.
- In 380 B.C., Plato wrote that physicians erred when they separated the soul from the body in providing healing and cures.
- It's important to find a discipline that most fits your lifestyle and personality, and then to create an approach that is uniquely yours.

CHAPTER EIGHT

Re-energize Your Life

The great world religions have superimposed themselves over
the indigenous shamanistic traditions that existed for hundreds
of thousands of years beforehand. Many of the sonic yogas of
Tibet and India already existed long before Buddhism. They
were very ancient. These exercises of chanting, rhythmical
bodily movement, rhythmical breathing, are very ancient
practices, which were incorporated into the great religions.

JILL PURCE, musician, writer, and artist;
"Sound in Mind & Body"

Before I get into some of the more common practices of meditation
and movement, I want to say something about breath and breathing. Breathing is, without question, our most important physical
function. To test this theory, try not breathing! Breathing is the regulator
that controls the metabolism and rids the lungs, glands, and organs of
wastes and poisons.

Deep, controlled breathing is a natural tranquilizer and rejuvenator.
Slowing down the rate of respiration also reduces the strain on the heart and
improves metabolic efficiency. By exercising the lungs and providing sufficient oxygen to the body, we increase resistance to the common cold and
ward off fatigue and sluggishness. The ability to process oxygen with maxi-
mum efficiency slows down the aging process.

Since breathing is an automatic process, we are often unaware that we are not breathing to full capacity. The breaths we take tend to be shallow and frequent, not surprising given that our lives are stressful and we rarely take time to slow down and pay attention to our bodies. Suppressed emotions can also restrict our breathing; we tense up to keep from feeling them or letting them out, often without even knowing that we're doing it.

This is why breath work is an important component of many of the practices I advocate. In yoga, for example, the specific exercise that focuses on awareness of the breath is referred to as *pranayama*. The movements that are linked to the in-breaths and out-breaths are referred to as *asanas*. The key to releasing stress and accessing a higher level of energy through yoga practice lies in the use of the breath. Such "conscious" breathing enables us to release our tensions and focus on what is going on physically during the movements. Over time, such practice sensitizes us to the quality of our thoughts and emotions; even spiritual awareness can deepen as our breath becomes a tool for change.

MEDITATION

For countless centuries, the ancient practice of meditation has been used to achieve mystical enlightenment and a direct experience of God. Traditional forms of meditation are as numerous as the religions and cultures from which they arose. In its earliest years meditation was practiced by shamans, who would go into trance to obtain knowledge or healing power on behalf of their tribe. Many African tribes still engage in a practice called "trance dancing," which is done in a group. It is similar to certain Native American rituals where participants dance all night in a foot-stomping ritual, also inducing a trance.

Other forms of meditation focus on breathing, the silent repetition of specific words or phrases, or particular energy centers of the body. The practice that we in the West are most familiar with is the sitting meditations of Buddhism, although meditation can be practiced while walking or standing, and some people even meditate when they exercise. Movement disciplines such as Chi Gung or yoga can also lead to a meditative state.

No matter which form you use, all effective meditations combine deep breathing, mindfulness, and stillness, leading to inner calm and alertness and a sense that you are connected with the center of your being. In practicing stillness, one develops the capacity for letting go of emotions and worries and the thoughts of the rational mind. In this silence, as we practice being the observer, we can more readily detach from our ego and see our world from another perspective. Once we've arrived in this more open, intuitive state, insights emerge that never would have made it through the chatter of our usual ways of thinking.

As noted above, there is a wide variety of meditation approaches available. Two of the more common—mantra meditation and walking meditation—are introduced below. Since meditation is ultimately a personal practice, choose whichever one is most appropriate to your personality and lifestyle. The important thing is to do it regularly, every day, even if for only a few minutes. As meditation becomes more of a routine, you will do it longer and more often, and the benefits will become more obvious.

MANTRA MEDITATION

The original Sanskrit meaning of *mantra* is "thought form," but it has come to mean a sacred name, word, or combination of words that can be as short as a single syllable or as long as several verses. Mantras are believed to have the capacity to transform consciousness when repeated silently in the mind. In fact, in its simplest form, mantra meditation is just sound vibrations—the sound of the mantra being repeated over and over again.

All the major religious traditions, including Buddhism, Sufism, Orthodox Christianity, and Hinduism (among others—see below), have their own mantras. In the 1960s, the Hindu teacher Maharishi Mahesh Yogi introduced mantra meditation to the U.S. through the practice of what is called Transcendental Meditation (TM), which leads to an extraordinary concentration achieved through repeating a meaningless sound. Those who are trained in TM are given their mantra by their meditation teacher, who urges them to keep the mantra a secret lest it lose its power.

Examples of mantras are:

• "Hail Mary" or "Ave Maria"	Catholic
• "Jesus"	Christian
• "Barukh attah Adonai" ("Blessed art thou, O Lord")	Jewish
• "Ribono shel olam" ("Lord of the universe")	Jewish/Hasidic
• "Allahu akbar" or "Allahu akbar min kulli shay" ("God is great")	Muslim
• "Om mani padme hum" ("Jewel in the lotus")	Buddhist
• "Rama Rama"	Hindu

The mantra one chooses can be the Sanskrit syllable "Om," the word "love," or any of those listed above, but it should promote a feeling of tranquility and be used consistently. Once you've chosen a specific mantra, it's best to stay with it and not switch around.

Recite your mantra quietly while paying attention to your breath. Let your awareness move inward. Let your breath, the mantra, and your awareness become one. The value of a mantra is that it can be used as part of a regular meditation practice or repeated in the midst of daily challenges or crises, such as when you're stuck in traffic or facing a difficult decision. Mantras can help you fall asleep or support you when you're angry, nervous, worried, afraid, or resentful. Simply repeat the mantra until the agitation or unwanted emotional response subsides. By chanting a mantra either out loud or quietly to yourself, you can actually change the state of your mind. With practice, a mantra becomes a silent and constant healing mental vibration.

Another form of mantra meditation is to quietly reflect on and repeat over and over an inspirational writing such as the Buddha's "Discourse on Good Will" or the Prayer of Saint Francis. Both of these are included in the *Words of Wisdom* section in Part Two of this book. Many of my clients keep these excerpts on their desks at work to remind them that they have the tools to deal with any difficult situation that arises.

WALKING MEDITATION

In Islam, and especially among the Sufi Orders, siyahat or "errance"—the action or rhythm of walking—was used as a technique for dissolving the attachments of the world and allowing men to lose themselves in God.

BRUCE CHATWIN,
The Songlines

A walking meditation can be one of the easiest forms of meditation, especially for those who find it difficult to sit still. It can often be a first step in incorporating meditation into your daily life. A walking meditation can be as simple as walking back and forth on a quiet path or even in your back yard. It should be practiced at a slow pace while paying attention to your breath and each step you take. The most obvious benefit of walking meditation is how it grounds you and helps you feel a greater connection to the earth.

Julia Cameron, a playwright and songwriter best known for her top selling books on the creative process, offers three tools for those who want to get in touch with their creativity: Morning Pages—journal-writing done first thing in the morning; Artist Date—a once-a-week solo outing to nurture the creative consciousness; and Walks.

Walks: The third pivotal creative tool is one that links together mind and body. The tool is walking. Like the Morning Pages and the Artist Date, it is deceptively simple, yet very powerful. A twenty-minute walk is long enough. An additional hour's walk once weekly is recommended. What does walking do? It nudges us out of our habitual thinking. It builds a bridge to higher consciousness. It allows us to access our intuition, to focus on solutions rather than problems.

JULIA CAMERON,
The Sound of Paper:
Starting from Scratch

"Labyrinth" walking is another form of meditation that was practiced by pilgrims in medieval times. A labyrinth is a spiritual tool designed to deepen the connection to whatever greater power one believes in. Participants walk a path through a geometrically precise and usually circular design that can be drawn onto floors or etched into the ground or even planted with hedges. The path into the center of the labyrinth represents the process of moving inward and releasing thoughts and emotions that no longer serve the spirit. Arrival in the center marks a time to be open, receptive, and empty of worry and concerns. It's an opportunity to seek guidance, direction, or a vision. Moving outward offers a chance to integrate the experience of the center and feel a greater connection with your own divinity.

It is believed that the first labyrinth was constructed for King Minos on the island of Crete. Labyrinths were adapted in Christian churches as part of the ancient Greco-Roman tradition, symbolizing the journey through life and its culmination in death. The most famous labyrinth in the world is the eleven-circuit design in Chartres Cathedral in France, which was built in 1220. Here in the U.S., interest in this simple form of meditation grows with books written about it, Web sites devoted to it, and labyrinths showing up everywhere, the most well-known of which may be in San Francisco's Grace Cathedral.

MOVING WITH YOGA AND CHI GUNG

The movement and stretching disciplines of yoga and Chi Gung stem from shamanic practices that are thousands of years old and were common across cultures. Tomb drawings in Egypt, for example, depict individuals in identical positions to those documented in ancient Indian texts. Even Islam and Christianity incorporated movements and poses in their practice of worship in the early years of their formation.

YOGA

Yoga is a 5000-year-old Indian science of physical and mental health that has become a mainstay in the health routines of the West. The word "yoga" means "union," as in "to be one with the divine," and represents the combined practice of postures (*asanas*), breath (*pranayama*), and stillness (meditation). The goal of yoga is to create harmony by integrating awareness of the mind, body, and spirit. The wide variety of different yoga postures, when properly practiced with correct breathing, engage the full natural range of movement of the human body. They balance the nervous system, promote the efficient functioning of the internal organs, and create an optimal state of health and well-being. Yoga has also been credited with the ability to sharpen the intellect and increase concentration. Millions believe it is the key to youthfulness, long life, vitality, and peace of mind.

It's not necessary to subscribe to any particular ideas of God in order to follow the yoga path. The practice of yoga only requires you to relax and let go, to move and be attentive to your movements, and to allow your breath to guide you. It also requires you to choose a specific yoga practice from the numerous variations, including Ashtanga, Bikram, Power Yoga, Viniyoga, and Kundalini. One primary distinction between them is the degree to which they prioritize for the body or the mind (though both are always present). Body-oriented yoga has become the most popular in the

West (just read any issue of *Yoga Journal*), but the more internal forms are slowly catching on.

Numerous books and videos teach basic as well as advanced movements, and classes are especially popular. Whichever form you choose, a good time to practice is either first thing in the morning—even fifteen or twenty minutes can motivate your spirit—or right after work, as an antidote to the stresses of the day. After-work yoga can also set the stage for a good night's sleep.

Having now studied and practiced yoga myself for more than twenty-five years, I find it promotes greater flexibility of both the body and the mind. I notice that individuals who are physically tense often have a corresponding mental rigidity. They're not as open to new ideas, and their ability to adapt to change may be constricted. This is unfortunate in today's environment of rapid change, where flexibility is the key to survival. When we feel fearful, angry, or resentful, our musculature automatically tightens; the same physical response occurs due to depression, lethargy, or apathy. In all these cases, yoga is an ideal remedy.

CHI GUNG

"Chi Gung" (*chee-gung*) means the "cultivation of chi"—working with the basic energy of life. It's an ancient Chinese system of exercises that gave rise to certain martial arts disciplines, but was also used for healing and preventing disease. The essence of Chi Gung can be understood by comparing the human body to a battery. Stress and destructive health habits act to dissipate the battery's charge; self-awareness and self-care maintain and improve the charge (or chi).

Chi Gung incorporates breathing, movement, and meditation to improve health and enhance vitality by cleansing, releasing, and circulating chi so that it permeates all the body's cells. Its practice can increase stamina, balance, and coordination, build strength, and even encourage spiritual awareness. It is used in Chinese medical institutions to combat disease: In a procedure similar to the ancient Christian practice of "laying on of hands," healing is accomplished through the transmission of positive energy from the Chi Gung practitioner to the patient.

Kenneth S. Cohen is one of the best-known Chi Gung teachers in the U.S. Cohen was a pioneer in bringing Chi Gung to the West and establishing the bridge between qigong (an alternative spelling for Chi Gung) and medical science. In his book, *The Way of Qigong: The Art and Science of Chinese Energy Healing*, he clearly describes the advantages of this practice:

> Qigong is a gentle yet rigorous program for working with our life energy through breathing and relaxation exercises, massage, visualization, meditation, and other natural methods. By practicing qigong, each one of us can learn to improve health and enhance vitality, by cleansing, gathering, releasing, and circulating qi so that it reaches all the body's cells. It's rather like acupuncture without needles—it's pleasurable to do, it costs nothing, and it's wonderfully life-enhancing.

I have practiced several forms of Chi Gung for more than fifteen years, and while I can't claim to have maintained a serious practice, I have gained an awareness of its value and seemingly miraculous results. One woman in particular stands out in my memory. She had been in a serious car accident and was told that she would never walk again. Yet when I met her (she was in her late sixties, two years after her accident), she seemed quite healthy and was practicing the form of Chi Gung—Shibashi Qigong— that I was also learning at the time. She considered her practice to have played a vital role in her recovery.

T'AI CHI CHIH

This "chi" is also used as translation for the Sanskrit word "prajna," which means wisdom in the greater sense. So the vital force, this intrinsic energy, is also the wisdom that is the deep-rooted source of intuition. A long-time practiser of T'ai Chi Chih will know well what the ancients meant when they said: "To unite the divine energy within me with the universal energy, that is the goal!"

JUSTIN STONE,
T'ai Chi Chih:
Joy Through Movement

T'ai Chi Chih was created by Justin F. Stone, who had been a teacher of T'ai Chi Ch'uan, the ancient and more traditional form of T'ai Chi that includes 108 different movements. Stone's observation, with which I heartily concur, is that the ancient practice of the 108 movements requires a discipline that few in the West can adhere to. A number of people I thought would benefit from T'ai Chi later told me that they found the practice too intimidating— some gave up after attending a single class!

T'ai Chi Chih, by comparison, consists of twenty movements which can readily be learned from an accredited teacher. For those who choose this practice, Stone offers a number of helpful guidelines. Of particular importance is to relax the shoulders and let the hands and wrists move in soft circular motions, as tension will keep the energy from flowing freely throughout the body. He states, "If you will remember to think of yourself as moving slow motion in a dream or swimming through heavy air, yet without exertion, you will have the idea of how to move." With time you will even be able to feel the denseness of the air around you during your practice.

Richard Brier, an accredited teacher of T'ai Chi Chih, states that the true miracles he observes are the life-changing attitudes in his students. "They become much more aware of the present, learn how to count their blessings, and are grateful to be alive." He also says that "people who practice openly, sincerely, and daily" achieve the greatest results. His mantra is "practice is power."

POWER NOTES

- By exercising your lungs through deep, controlled breathing, you increase resistance to the common cold and ward off fatigue and sluggishness.
- All effective meditation practices combine deep breathing, mindfulness, and stillness, leading to inner calm and alertness and a sense that you are connected with the center of your being.
- Mantras are believed to have the capacity to transform consciousness when repeated silently in the mind.
- Walking meditation can be one of the easiest forms of meditation, especially for those who find it difficult to sit still.
- The movement and stretching disciplines of yoga and Chi Gung stem from shamanic practices that are thousands of years old.
- The goal of yoga is to create harmony by integrating awareness of the mind, body, and spirit, and millions believe it is the key to youthfulness, long life, vitality, and peace of mind.
- The essence of Chi Gung can be understood by comparing the human body to a battery. Stress and destructive health habits act to dissipate the battery's charge; self-awareness and self-care maintain and improve the charge (or chi).

CHAPTER NINE

Tune in with Sound

"We ourselves are rhythm," wrote Hazrat Inayat Khan. "The beating of our heart, the pulse throbbing in our wrist or head, our circulation, the working of the whole mechanisms of our body is rhythmic." As a doctor, I know this to be true. As a healer, I believe that our bodies resonate with the sounds produced by our voices, most vividly perhaps when we are in tune with the sound of the singing bowls. And as we resonate on a cellular level, we begin to heal physically, spiritually, and emotionally.

MITCHELL L. GAYNOR, M.D.,
Sounds of Healing:
A Physician Reveals the
Therapeutic Power of
Sound, Voice, and Music

Dr. Mitchell Gaynor is one of the new doctors pioneering the use of the ancient power of sound to bring about healing. He is Director of Medical Oncology and Integrative Medicine at the Strang-Cornell Cancer Prevention Center, which is affiliated with New York Hospital. In his book he shares how he has used chanting, music, and quartz crystal bowls to treat patients since 1991. His results have been remarkable; many of his patients have gone into remission and become cancer-free.

The basic principle behind sound healing is that all matter in the universe— including every organ in the human body— is in a state of energetic vibration.

If we live "out of tune," if our energy bodies aren't in balance, then we'll attract the same kind of energy from the world around us. Angry people, for example, will draw other angry people to them. In the same way, when we live in harmony within ourselves and with the natural world, we attract people and opportunities that resonate with those same positive qualities.

Since sound is energy and different sounds resonate with different energies, it is logical to see that the sounds around us can have either positive or negative impacts on our physical, emotional, mental, and spiritual health. Imagine the sound of music that lifts your spirits and helps you feel renewed and refreshed. The right tunes can connect us with our own joy, give us hope, and even inspire us to go out and do great things. Think of how uplifting and energizing are the themes from *Chariots of Fire*, *Flashdance*, or *Rocky*. Recall how calm and at peace you feel when you listen to Pachelbel's famous Canon in D minor (remember the movie *10*?). We all have our own favorites.

On the other hand, "noise"—defined as sound that actually decreases physical energy and inner harmony when it reaches a certain level of intensity—is considered one of the most significant contributors to stress in the modern world. Noise has been implicated in a variety of physical conditions, from ulcers, migraines, impotence, and vertigo to reduced resistance to infections, shrinkage of the thymus gland, and swelling of the adrenal gland. Don Campbell, a pioneer in promoting a higher awareness of the impacts of sound on our quality of life, writes in his bestselling book The Mozart Effect that high levels of unpleasant sounds cause blood vessels to constrict, increase blood pressure, pulse, and respiratory rates, and cause the blood's magnesium level to fall. Long-term exposure to noise causes ear damage, disrupts the central nervous system, and creates perceptual distortions in hearing and possibly in the other senses.

In his book, Campbell discusses numerous examples of how sound and music have stimulated improvements in job performance at work:

> The evidence is in: Music in the workplace has been shown to raise performance levels and productivity by reducing stress and tension, masking irritating sounds, and contributing to a sense of privacy.

(A side benefit of the sense of well-being—it can foster reduced health-care costs.) Forty-three of the world's fifty largest industrial companies provide music to employees.

HEALING WITH SOUND

Sound healing, then, is pretty much what it says—the use of sound to heal and rebalance. Some scientists and medical practitioners believe that illness and disease result when some part of the body begins to vibrate at a frequency that's out of sync with its natural rhythm, and that certain sound vibrations can restore equilibrium. It has been scientifically proven that slow, deep breathing will reduce the heart rate and brain activity, and that sounding a single note or mantra like "Om" will create a deeper state of relaxation. Such sounding is called "toning," done to reduce stress or realign the energy field. Healthy sound vibrations are like tuning forks that enable you to return to your own true nature. Using sound in conjunction with breath and visualization can be an extremely powerful and transformative experience.

In most indigenous cultures, toning or making vocal sounds, along with drumming, are essential parts of healing. The use of singing, toning, and chanting to improve health and alter awareness has been practiced for thousands of years in a number of religious traditions, including those of the Greeks, Egyptians, Islamic Sufis, and Native Americans, as well as in Sanskrit and Christian Gregorian chanting and Tibetan rituals. Chinese medicine uses Taoist meditations that involve deep breathing and mantras comprised of sacred syllables chanted in deep, low-pitched tones to restore balance to the body-mind system.

Like ancient shamans and Indian Vedic seers, Jewish mystics have long understood how sound affects our bodies. The Jewish mystical tradition of Kabbalah incorporates chants into its meditation and visualization practice. The Kabbalists believe that sound and music were instrumental in the origin of the universe.

The Many Benefits of Sound

Although the research on sound healing is still accumulating, enough reports and evidence have come in to show that this can be an enormously effective treatment for a wide variety of disorders and disease, psychological as well as physical. On a physical level, sound therapy:

- is being used successfully in many parts of the world to reduce stress, prevent illness, and alleviate pain.
- is proving effective in lowering blood pressure.
- is being used to control hyperactivity in children and to facilitate healthy brain organization and learning skills in both children and adults who have learning disabilities.
- elicits a state of tranquility in people who are feeling agitated and apprehensive, even stimulating intuition and increased creativity.
- is being used as a meditative stimulus to help treat those with a life-threatening disease.

"I'm convinced," says Dr. Gaynor, "that when my patients use sound and meditation to achieve a sense of peace and spiritual ease, they also strengthen their bodies, which enables them to handle the side effects of whatever medical treatment they're undergoing and advance the process of healing—emotional and immunological—that is as essential to their recovery as any drug or therapy I might offer them."

On a more psychological level, sound therapy:

- facilitates the release of painful and destructive emotions such as anger and fear and the ache and grief of a traumatic experience.
- helps to eliminate depression.
- enables you to be more open to joy, laughter, and love, and to extend forgiveness and compassion toward others and yourself.
- helps to release your resistance to change.
- can reconnect you to the source of your inner power and energy.

Sound is one of the most transformative healing energies on the planet, capable of restoring balance and harmony to individuals as well as to physical environments. It is also one of the most readily accessible. Just pop in a CD, tap your Tibetan bells, or take a walk along the beach or a stream to experience how powerful sound can be.

MUSICAL INSTRUMENTS
THAT HEAL

People of indigenous communities have used rattles, drums, and bells for thousands of years to promote good health. In her book *The Four-Fold Way*, Angeles Arrien notes that sticks and clicking sounds are used to break harmful family or cultural patterns; the rattle is used for cleansing and purification and to call back lost parts of our essence; the drum is used to pay attention to what we value or what has heart and meaning for us; the bell has traditionally been used to call us back to our authentic purpose.

Therapists and psychotherapists are now using drums to help release the emotional pain of stress disorders and promote the health of at-risk adolescents, stressed-out employees, and people who have Alzheimer's and Parkinson's diseases. Among modern Western physicians, the use of quartz crystal bowls as instruments of healing is also becoming a popular method of sound therapy. When the rim of such a bowl is smoothly encircled with a mallet, the powerful sound vibrations create a delicate internal massage of the cells, enabling a patient's body to restore its own harmonic frequency. In this way, the individual's intuition is enhanced and a relaxed, meditative state is induced.

For anyone exposed to the daily noise of telephones, traffic, sirens, construction, commercials, or even just the constant hum of a computer, listening to the tones that ring from a crystal bowl is a wonderful relief. And the experience involves more than just hearing it; since sound is vibration, you feel it physically. A crystal bowl can help you to quickly reach a place of deep tranquility.

THE HEALING POWER OF THE VOICE

The voice is the most readily available instrument of transformation. It influences all the levels of your being: your emotional and mental states, your spiritual awareness, and your physical body. The study of how sound, language, and music affect the brain is known as "psychoacoustics." Singing, toning, and chanting have been proven to affect the emotional circuitry of the brain, inducing profound states of relaxation and even improving our learning abilities. Shamanism and mystical traditions have used sounds and multiple overtones to invoke different deities and energy forces for the purpose of balancing the chakras or etheric centers.

"The use of chanting, where the voice is often mid-way between speech and singing, is common to shamanism," writes Caitlin Matthews in *Singing the Soul Back Home: Shamanism in Daily Life*. She continues:

> Specific chants are taught to shamans by their spirits; these chants are
> regarded as sacred regalia, to be held in trust by the shaman and her
> successors inalienably. Chants of healing, of welcoming the spirits, or
> of calling upon the powers of the universe soon become part of the
> personal sacred regalia of any walker between the worlds. These are
> the songs by which you will restore the human voice to its rightful
> task and sing the wandering soul back home.

One of the pioneers in the field of sound, toning, and chanting is Jill Purce, a London musician, writer, and artist. Purce believes that the prevalence of cynicism and alienation in Western society is a result of our literally having no "chant" in our lives. She states that "To keep people 'in tune' is to keep them healthy." Her aim is to re-en-chant the world and create more magic through people chanting together again. She explains in one of her many informative articles:

> The Tibetans talk about the human being in three ways. They talk of
> body, of voice, and of mind. These have three locations. The position

86

for 'body' is in the head. The 'voice' is in the throat and the position of 'mind' is in the heart. For Tibetans there is no identity between mind and brain, as in the West. So the voice acts as an intermediary between the subtle realm of mind and the more physical realm of body. So it is seen as a bridge between the material and the immaterial.

One of Purce's primary forms is the Mongolian overtone chanting that she learned at Gyuto Tantric College from a Tibetan chantmaster. Overtoning utilizes a single note that is modulated by shaping the mouth so that high, bell-like sounds are heard above the bass note. It has been said that when you listen to this type of chanting, it evokes the music of the cosmos.

Marilyn's Story

After suffering for several months with near debilitating pains in my ab-domen that no treatment could relieve, a dear friend and world-famous therapist and sound healer came to visit me. Noticing my discomfort and lis-tening to my description of my problem, he offered me a session that very af-ternoon. I was asked to close my eyes and "just experience the sounds." Using a singing bowl to accompany his incredible four-octave-range voice, this gifted man created a vibration around me that, with startling sudden-ness, entered my body precisely in the area of pain, lightly vibrating every raw inch. I don't know how much time passed before I realized that I had drifted into an altered state. When I opened my eyes the pain was gone. The pain has never returned, and I feel blessed to have experienced this ancient and familiar healing.

THE SOUNDS THAT CONNECT US

While there is insufficient scientific evidence on the healing effects of sound, most individuals in the field of sound work agree that in the near future, when science and spirituality merge, it will become apparent that changing our vibrational rates is the key to transformation and well-being, and that the use of sound may be the most effective tool for doing so. The language that all cultures and possibly all species understand is rhythm and sound; it has a great capacity for uniting us as fellow citizens of the planet.

POWER NOTES

- If we live "out of tune," if our energy bodies aren't in balance, then we'll attract the same kind of energy from the world around us.
- Since sound is energy and different sounds resonate with different energies, the sounds around us can have either positive or negative impacts on our physical, emotional, mental, and spiritual health.
- "Noise"—defined as sound that actually decreases physical energy and inner harmony when it reaches a certain level of intensity—is considered one of the most significant contributors to stress in the modern world.
- Some scientists and medical practitioners believe that illness and disease result when some part of the body begins to vibrate at a frequency that's out of sync with its natural rhythm, and that certain sound vibrations can restore equilibrium.
- In most indigenous cultures, toning or making vocal sounds, along with drumming, is an essential part of healing. The use of singing, toning, and chanting to improve health and alter awareness has been practiced for thousands of years in many religious traditions.
- Singing, toning, and chanting have been proven to affect the emotional circuitry of the brain, inducing profound states of relaxation and even improving our learning abilities.
- In the near future, when science and spirituality merge, it will become apparent that changing our vibrational rates is the key to transformation and well-being, and that the use of sound may be the most effective tool for doing so.

BRING BALANCE AND HARMONY TO YOUR LIFE

CHAPTER TEN

Harmony and Balance

Every space has energy. Your home is not only a composite of
materials assembled for shelter. Every cubic centimeter of it,
whether solid or seemingly empty space, is composed of infinite
energy. When you enter a space that makes you immediately
feel light or uplifted, or walk into a room where the atmosphere
leaves you feeling depleted and drained, you are responding to
the energy of the environment.

DENISE LINN, *Space Clearing:*
Show to Purify and Create
Harmony in Your Home

W e all want our lives to be productive, rewarding, and balanced, and our environments to be beautiful and harmonious. Yet few people enjoy a lifestyle that gives them this
sense of wholeness, nor do they work or live in physical spaces conducive
to such an experience. The design of the buildings and spaces we inhabit affects our energy, creativity, effectiveness, and sense of harmony—or lack
thereof. Ideally, buildings should be situated and built to harmonize with
the natural environment; interiors and exteriors should also reflect some aspect of the natural world. Churches should not be the only places where we
can practice inner reflection and regain a sense of peace.

In ancient times, sacred sites such as Stonehenge in England and others
in Egypt, Greece, and Malta reflected humanity's spiritual vision and its

connection with the cycles of the seasons and the natural world. Before religion as we now know and practice it, the power of nature and its life-giving and death-wielding aspects were honored and revered. Today we have lost that sense of mystery and intimacy we had with Mother Earth. Angeles Arrien believes that people who don't spend at least an hour outside every day will experience soul loss. If that's true, then most urban dwellers are heading in that direction—alienated and confused, and not really sure why.

Creating a harmonizing balance in our lives is as much art as science, and there is no one-size-fits-all solution. It requires time for reflection and a change in perspective. We may need to learn new disciplines and techniques or take action in a new direction. When it comes to the physical spaces we live and work in, no less of an effort is needed, because their influence on us is deceptively strong. Fortunately, there is much that we can do, and one of the best approaches can be found in the ancient practice of *feng shui* ("fung-shway").

BALANCING THE INNER AND OUTER

Feng shui, also known as "the art of placement," combines geophysical observation, psychology, religion, folklore, art, nature, and common sense. Its origin dates back 3000 years in China, spreading 2000 years later to Japan and other Asian countries. In Europe, a more simplified version came to be known as geomancy. Here in the U.S., feng shui has become an increasingly popular tool for people who are looking to change their lives and more successfully reach their goals and dreams.

Literally translated, feng shui means "wind and water." It evolved from the simple observation that people are affected, for good or ill, by their surroundings and environment—by the layout and orientation of workplaces and homes and the objects within them. Consequently, by changing your surroundings you can change your life. Put another way, in order to bring about a certain desired internal reality—say, the contentment felt when manifesting wealth or knowing you're "on the right track"—it helps to make changes to your external reality. (This principle also works in the opposite direction!) We do this by realigning our homes and offices so that they are in harmony with the greater forces of nature and the creative energies of the universe.

Underlying the philosophy of feng shui is the principle of yin and yang—the positive and negative forces of energy—and the belief that, when one is dominant over the other, an imbalance occurs. Feng shui acts to correct that imbalance.

In simpler terms, feng shui can be thought of as a process of goal setting. Its practice symbolizes what you want to create in your life. In my personal experience, the changes that occur when one follows the principles of feng shui are chiefly due to the strength of the intention and commitment to the process. The feng shui design known as the *bagua* identifies eight key areas of a house that correspond to the primary areas of life where important decisions are made. Those eight areas and the corresponding colors commonly associated with them are:

1. RED: Fame/Recognition/Reputation
2. PINK: Marriage/Relationships/Romance/Friends
3. WHITE: Children/Creativity/Future Projects
4. GRAY: Helpful People/Travel/Neighbors
5. BLACK: Career/Prospects/Beginnings
6. BLUE: Knowledge/Spirituality/Education/Wisdom
7. GREEN: Family/Past/Health
8. PURPLE: Prosperity/Wealth/Accumulation

THE BAGUA

While many comprehensive books have been written on how to approach feng shui and the bagua, the basic steps are these:

- Identify what you want to change in your life or what you're committed to creating that is currently not present.

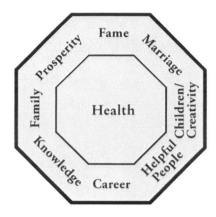

- Identify what in your life isn't working or is creating a problem for you.
- Identify the colors and areas of your home that feel "off" or uncomfortable.
- Determine what obvious problems exist in these areas, for example, too much clutter or dust or too many negative symbols.
- Choose positive symbols (in art, books, etc.) that reflect your desired change.
- Write out what you're committed to doing in the eight areas of your life.
- Fold or roll the paper and tie it with a beautiful ribbon or otherwise preserve it in a way that honors the power and hope that it holds for you.

The reason this process works is that most of us are so busy and our lives so full that we spend very little time reflecting on what's truly important to us and what we're committed to creating. I have practiced and studied feng shui and geomancy for more than 15 years. I know that these practices work and can produce dramatic changes. While some of these changes may appear miraculous, it is just common sense that if you simplify your life and get clear about your goals, you'll more readily manifest what you want.

The Manifest Your Desires action plan in Part Two will help you get even more clear about how to improve an existing situation, although the goal-setting practice of feng shui is a good first step toward achieving anything you want to do in your life.

A Feng Shui Convert

Many individuals believe that feng shui is so ancient and based on so many superstitions that the practice would not be relevant to their busy and modern lifestyle. When I started working with Robert, he felt the same, and was even put off that I would suggest such an idea. Robert had contacted me to discuss how I might support him in increasing his business revenue. He was a successful entrepreneur in the healthcare industry. Over a period of five years, he had positioned himself as one of the leaders in his industry and was sought after for speaking engagements and consulting projects for Fortune 500 companies. When we sat down to look at his current revenue and compared it to his projections, it was clear that his cash flow wasn't the problem, it was the receivables. The challenge of juggling a demanding schedule of client support, traveling and speaking was leaving him little time to manage collections. His "successful" life had turned into a "chaotic" life with no room for planning or looking ahead. Because Robert was bright and analytical and spent most of his time thinking and creating, I felt a hands-on feng shui approach would be the best place to start as it was so contrary to his usual way of managing his life and his business.

His office and that of his two assistants were crammed with documents, boxes, industry magazines and newsletters, and numerous stacks of reading material. When I asked about some of the various piles, he indicated he needed to review anything before he could throw it out. I knew that unless he cleared the clutter in his office and created systems that would make managing his life easier, the piles would still be there in five years. He agreed that in two weeks he'd create order in his office. When I returned two weeks later the office had experienced quite a transformation. He told me that he'd worked evenings and both weekends going through old articles and client memos he was intending to file. He enrolled both of his assistants in the process of getting organized, and their work spaces had changed remarkably.

The next step was developing systems to prevent him from getting buried in paper work again. Once we had that in place, he and his staff were ready to implement some deeper "feng shui" changes to the office. While they worked on rearranging the energy in their environment, I created a system for tracking revenue. By the time I returned to his office 30 days later, 60 percent of his outstanding receivables had been deposited in the bank.

CLEARING CLUTTER

> Clutter accumulates when energy stagnates and, likewise, energy stagnates when clutter accumulates. So the clutter begins as a symptom of what is happening with you in your life and then becomes a part of the problem itself because the more of it you have, the more stagnant energy it attracts to itself.
>
> KAREN KINGSTON,
> *Clear Your Clutter with Feng Shui:*
> *Free Yourself from Physical, Mental,*
> *Emotional, and Spiritual Clutter Forever*

One of the most valuable principles of feng shui is the practice of cleaning one's house and going through all of the files, storage spaces, and personal belongings. All matter has energy and a certain feel to it (compare, for example, a clean sink to a dirty sink), and you may find yourself surrounded by furniture, clothes, knick-knacks, and so on that feel old or no longer relevant to your life. Clearing this clutter and letting go of items you don't need is a way of creating space for new opportunities to come into your life.

Holding on to family heirlooms, for instance, although they are beautiful and of great value, may be draining your energy if those keepsakes don't inspire you. Immersing yourself in reminders of your regrets, failures, disappointments, or painful memories will not contribute to personal growth. Hanging on to something out of a sense of obligation, such as a gift you don't like but feel you must keep so you won't hurt someone's feelings, is a big energy depleter.

Not surprisingly, individuals who surround themselves with lots of "stuff" tend to lack focus. This often characterizes those who live in the fast lane, juggling multiple commitments, responsibilities, and distractions. Instead of determining which areas of their lives are most important and deserve the greatest amount of time and attention, they scatter their energies in so many directions that no one area is successful. Unfortunately, we often become so accustomed to our lifestyle and surroundings that we don't realize how negatively they might be affecting our energy and ability to get control of our personal and professional lives.

A good rule of thumb: Keep only those objects that make you feel energized, happy, or joyful. Some questions to consider when reflecting on your home environment:

- How does the "container" I live in support my intentions?
- How does my home make me feel? Tired, overwhelmed, inspired, at peace?
- What objects need to be given away?
- Where in my home is the best location to create a place of contemplation, reflection, and relaxation?

Once you begin rearranging your personal belongings and giving some of them away, you'll experience firsthand how material objects and possessions can affect your energy and how you view yourself and the world around you. If you already have an energy practice (e.g., yoga, meditation, or Chi Gung), attending to your physical surroundings will enhance those efforts. An unintended by-product of creating a home that "feels good" is that it will also enhance its value. In my experience, buyers will pay at least ten percent above the market value of a home just because it feels "right" to them.

HOME AS SANCTUARY

Finding sanctuary amid life's chaos is a prerequisite to achieving greater life balance. *The American Heritage Dictionary* describes sanctuary as: 1. A sacred place, such as a church, temple, or mosque; or 2. A place of refuge, asylum, or protection.

What I mean by sanctuary is a place that feels nourishing, comforting, and inspiring. I don't decorate my home like a church, but I view it as a sacred place and try to replicate the feeling and experience I get when I sit in a place of worship. I'm even discerning about the people I invite there! Whether you live in a small apartment or a sprawling house, your environment should inspire you and remind you of what's important in your life—what you hold most sacred.

Creating a sanctuary from the stresses of work and the "noises" of the outside world helps you to slow down and feel more grounded. Surrounding yourself with beauty and inspirational objects keeps you in touch with your dreams and your purpose. Achieving a feeling of sanctuary is not related to airtight security (i.e., fences, gates, multiple locks on doors), nor does it have to do with how much money is spent on furniture or personal belongings. A multi-million-dollar home can be devoid of a feeling of sanctuary if it's designed and decorated to impress rather than to create a sense of welcome and comfort.

The first thing you'll notice when you walk into someone's home is how it feels—the quality of energy that dominates it. Homes that nurture the soul come in all shapes and sizes. Even an "inner-city" home can evoke feelings of harmony and a connection with nature through the use of plants, flowers, a simple fountain, a fireplace, or a collection of natural objects such as rocks, driftwood, or pine cones. The colors, textures, and materials chosen, whether natural or synthetic, can further contribute to the creation of a nurturing and inviting space. We all have different lifestyles and personal needs, and so the variety of "home-as-sanctuary" environments is endless. Each will have a personality and a character that embodies the essence of its inhabitants. Its capacity to reflect peace and beauty reflects the ability of its occupants to live comfortably in the world.

In creating such an environment, it's more important that you imprint your own vision of harmony than hire a professional designer, decorator, or feng shui practitioner to advise you. As talented as they can be, they may leave you with a reflection of their own tastes and energy rather than your own. A newly designed space won't be nurturing or complete until you've personalized it and made it yours. A home is not only a symbol of what you value in life but also of the state of your consciousness. Rearranging your home is like rearranging your consciousness; the process itself will be as transformative personally as it will be for the physical space you live in.

CREATING PLACES OF SOLITUDE

In our fast-paced environment, designating a specific place for personal solitude and reflection within your home will help you maintain a sense of inner peace. If you're married or living with someone or simply sharing a space with others, it's even more essential to create such a place.

The size of this place of reflection isn't important. It might be the corner of a room where you can meditate or listen to inspiring music. Maybe you've turned a large closet into a meditation room or designated a bookshelf as a place for things that you value. The top of an old dresser may be the perfect surface upon which to create an altar. Altars, usually thought of in a religious context, can also be a place to honor what has meaning for you. Photographs of people and places, favorite objects, incense, stones, anything that evokes your own special sense of what is sacred, can remind you of how fulfilling such a feeling is. Did you ever notice how often children create special places in their rooms for their most cherished treasures?

SIMPLIFYING YOUR LIFE

It's hard to manifest what we want in life or to shift our reality if we're not grounded. Yet every day we seem to be further entrenched in our heads, analyzing, rationalizing, planning, and surviving. When you learn how to slow down, simplify, and create an environment that nourishes your spirit, your life will become more balanced, harmonious, and fulfilling. From a more centered and focused state of mind, you can make wiser decisions. You'll then be able to discover the nature of your own particular genius, stop trying to conform to other people's models, and learn to be your authentic, individuated self.

POWER NOTES

- Creating a harmonizing balance in your life is as much art as science, and there is no one-size-fits-all solution.
- The design of buildings and physical spaces affects your energy, creativity, effectiveness, and sense of harmony—or lack thereof.
- Feng shui, also known as "the art of placement," combines geophysical observation, psychology, religion, folklore, art, nature, and common sense.
- By changing your surroundings, you can change your life.
- Underlying the philosophy of feng shui is the principle of yin and yang—the positive and negative forces of energy—and the belief that, when one is dominant over the other, an imbalance occurs.
- It is just common sense that if you simplify your life and get clear about your goals, you'll more readily manifest what you want.
- We often become so accustomed to our lifestyle and surroundings that we don't realize how negatively they might be affecting our energy and ability to get control of our personal and professional life.
- An unintended by-product of creating a home that "feels good" is that it will also enhance its value.
- Creating a sanctuary from the stresses of work and the "noises" of the outside world helps you to slow down and feel more grounded.
- Surrounding yourself with beauty and inspirational objects keeps you in touch with your dreams and your purpose.
- Rearranging your home is like rearranging your consciousness; the process itself will be as transformative personally as it will be for the physical space you live in.
- When you learn how to slow down, simplify, and create an environment that nourishes your spirit, your life will become more balanced, harmonious, and fulfilling.

CHAPTER ELEVEN

Intentions and Commitments

The idea is to seek a vision that gives you purpose in life and
then to implement that vision. The vision by itself is one
half, one part, of a process. It implies the necessity of living
that vision, otherwise the vision will sink back into itself.

LEWIS P. JOHNSON

We live in a time when it's easy to feel powerless, without control over our daily lives let alone our future. This feeling of powerlessness can cause us to become disillusioned with careers, hamstrung by stress-related illness, disappointed with transient relationships, and even paralyzed by a general confusion of self-purpose. Traditional methods of coping with stress and the challenges of the modern world—denying your fears, taking the latest drugs, working even harder—simply aren't working. And yet this crisis of overwhelm, this period of breakdown, also presents an opportunity to broaden your perspective and create a new personal vision, one more closely aligned with your dreams and motivating life purpose.

THE PATH OF MASTERY

In my work, I have observed unique characteristics possessed by those who are advancing on what I would describe as the "path of mastery." Such people embody certain qualities that allow them to make healthy changes in their lives and a positive difference in the lives of others. This path of mastery and inner wisdom has also been called the path of the "way-shower"—a person who has the ability to shed light on new realities for others. This development of mastery is not an event but a journey.

Individuals in touch with their own power and mastery possess the following traits:

- Their commitments, intentions, and actions are clear and focused.
- They have a strong understanding of their purpose.
- They experience a heightened sense of awareness and certainty about life and their decisions.
- They are clear about their strengths, gifts, and unique qualities.
- They feel aligned and in synergy with others and the natural environment.
- They draw from specific sources of inspiration.
- They have a daily practice of prayer or meditation.
- They experience a strong sense of intuitive inner knowing, as if they are being guided by a universal or divine presence

Our lives are a reflection of what we are committed to and what we give energy to. Your commitments are what you value and believe is of greatest importance. They are the areas where you put your time, energy, and focus. Figuring out what you are committed to doesn't have to be difficult. The first step is to look at how and where you live and work and the quality of your health, your relationships, and your finances; these outcomes reflect the commitments you've made, for good or ill. If you are financially stressed or limited, then that is your commitment. If you are ill or suffering from aches and pains, then that is what you are committed to—or to those things that give rise to such results. Sometimes it's not a pleasant realization, something I have learned from experience. Who will admit that they are committed to poverty or illness? Looking honestly at your life is a challenge. If you don't like what you see or the way you are living, ask yourself why you keep repeating the same types of actions that bring the same undesirable results—What are the "payoffs"?—and start making new commitments and different choices.

The kinds of commitments you've made also have more subtle characteristics: your speech patterns and use of words; your thoughts, feelings, and emotions; how you dress and the colors you choose. All of these combined emit a quality of energy, a communication to the world about who you are and what's important to you. For those who have developed the skills of an observer, such clues tell volumes about a person within minutes of contact. They are also clues for you as to the choices you've made and whether they represent the direction you really want to take in life.

Patty's Story

When I met Patty, she was married and had just moved to a lovely home in the country with a breathtaking view of the hills and surrounding vineyard. Both she and her husband, Peter, had worked hard to achieve this. Peter then decided to work part-time as a realtor to supplement their retirement income and to meet new people. Patty had no interest in continuing her banking career but did have a desire to become active in her new community. Due to their impressive business backgrounds, they were both invited to join the governing boards of several local groups, and within a few years each of them was serving on three boards. The time commitment to these organizations, combined with Peter's part-time career and visits from their friends and children, was becoming too much. Their goal had been to work hard, make a lot of money, and move to the country. But now that they were living in their dream house, they were not only exhausted but felt there was no meaning to their lives. They had spent 30 years working in the corporate world and were skilled at planning, financial projections, and setting goals, but they had never focused on setting personal goals.

When we started working with the Manifest Your Desires action plan, they realized that all of their goals had been possession-oriented—they had-

n't taken the time to consider what would really make them happy or what they were passionate about. Within months, both had reduced their local volunteer work and Patty had decided to start a part-time business. She realized that the aspect of her job in corporate America that she enjoyed the most was teaching people how to manage their investments. She kept the business small and chose not to work more than 20 hours a week. When we were working on her Lifework Plan, she realized that she wanted to travel more but felt that their budget couldn't accommodate it. So one of the purposes in starting her new business was to generate enough extra money to enable her and Peter to travel to a different foreign country every year for at least four weeks. She even incorporated her commitment into her new business, informing her clients that she would be unavailable each fall during the month of September.

What are you committed to changing in your life? How will you do it?

INTENTIONS, ACTIONS, AND COMMITMENTS

My actions are my only true belonging: I cannot escape the consequences of my actions. My actions are the ground on which I stand.

THE BUDDHA
(c.500 BC), India

We've all had the experience of making decisions and taking actions that later turned out to be the wrong choice relative to a particular goal or desire. When this happens, we are usually confused because we thought we were doing the right thing.

The truth is that at such times, we aren't that clear about our intentions and may not even know what our real intentions are. An individual without clear intentions is like a rudderless boat. Sometimes the intentions we think we have are connected to unconscious motivations that we aren't aware of.

In a relationship, for example, we may *intend* to be supportive and loving, but lurking underneath and over-riding that intention may be a desire to always be right and to have it our way. In another example, you may *intend* to make more money, but at a deeper level believe that people who make money are crooks or don't deserve the money they do make—a clear impediment to manifesting those goals.

Changing these patterns is a challenge, but people do it all the time. The exercises in Part Two of the book will get you started on the "right intentioned" path. And in *Living in Balance: A Dynamic Approach for Creating Harmony and Wholeness in a Chaotic World*, authors Joel and Michelle Levey draw from the wisdom of the indigenous peoples for advice on keeping focused and intentional on a daily basis:

The elders of the Seneca nation traditionally encouraged their people to reflect on four essential questions in order to determine if they were living in balance with their world. As you read each of these four questions, pause to reflect and honestly answer each one:

- Are you happy living how you are living and doing what you are doing?
- Is what you are doing adding to the confusion?
- What are you doing to further peace and contentment in your own life and in the world?
- How will you be remembered after you are gone—either in absence or in death?

Incorporating daily review of your intentions into your schedule, even for just 15 or 20 minutes (ideally at the same time each day), will give you the foundation and centering required to begin making real changes in your life and in the culture and environments you live and work in. When you passionately focus on your intentions in this way, you start tapping into your personal power. Once you commit to a new and positive direction, unforeseen events will occur to support you in your new endeavors.

So consider this: If you were to ask yourself one question that would help you stay focused and on track on a daily basis, what would it be?

FINDING BALANCE

Finding balance amid the chaos is an art, not a science, and each person's path will be different. It requires time out for reflection and a change in perspective. You may need to learn new disciplines and techniques to empower your body and mind. It may require that you get support to change your lifestyle and take action in a new direction.

Every day we're further entrenched in our heads, analyzing, rationalizing, planning, and surviving, often with a nagging sense that something vital is missing that will help us feel more complete and at peace. When your life is out of balance in this way you begin to feel disconnected, and can be unaware that you're making poor personal and business decisions. Failing to restore a sense of balance takes you further away from your goals and dreams and an experience of meaningfulness and satisfaction. Often past traumas or disappointments get in the way, perhaps causing you to lose your self-esteem and creating self-doubts about your worthiness. Everyone, no matter how rich, successful, or famous, is subject to feelings of low self-esteem or a belief that they aren't "good enough."

One of my favorite ways to gain perspective on decisions or life choices is to ask myself the same question that the Seneca elders posed: *Am I contributing to a greater degree of harmony in myself and the world with this action, or adding to the chaos and confusion?* Your life doesn't need to be filled with relentless challenge, obstacle, and crisis. You have the ability to live a full, rewarding, and productive life despite the turmoil around you. Because chaotic times cause us to question our priorities and modes of thinking, they represent an opportunity to assess what's really important—what we most value in life.

SIMPLIFICATION

In my personal experience as well as in my observations of clients, I've seen that one of the most valuable practices one can adopt in the quest for balance and harmony is simplification. This is an especially challenging yet necessary task given the busyness of living in our world. In the United States, the shift in the last century from a rural to a more urban and indoor environment has challenged our ability to process the increasing pace of cultural and technological change. The more technologically advanced we become, the more disconnected we get from our bodies and our basic natures. We spend most of our time in our heads and less time connecting to the earth. While humans once lived largely outdoors, connected to the cycles of nature, urban dwellers now spend at least 75 percent of their time indoors. It's hard to manifest what we want in life or to shift our reality if we aren't more grounded, physically as well as energetically.

POWER NOTES

- The path of mastery and inner wisdom has also been called the path of the "way-shower"—a person who has the ability to shed light on new realities for others.
- Our lives are a reflection of what we are committed to and what we give energy to.
- An individual without intention is like a rudderless boat.
- Once you commit to a new and positive direction, unforeseen events will occur to support you in your new endeavors.
- Finding balance amid the chaos is an art, not a science, and each person's path will be different.
- Because chaotic times cause us to question our priorities and modes of thinking, they represent an opportunity to assess what's really important—what we most value in life.
- One of the most valuable practices one can adopt in the quest for balance and harmony is simplification.
- It's hard to manifest what you want in life or to shift your reality if you aren't more grounded, physically as well as energetically.

CREATE YOUR PATH TO HEALTH AND WELLNESS

CHAPTER TWELVE

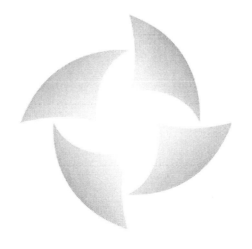

Energy Medicine and Healing

We are already whole. Underneath our fears and worries,
unaffected by the many layers of our conditioning and actions,
is a peaceful core. The work of healing is in peeling away
the barriers of fear that keep us unaware of our true nature
of love, peace, and rich interconnection with the web of
life. Healing is the rediscovery of who we are and who we
have always been.

JOAN BORYSENKO, PH.D.,
Healers on Healing

Over 158 million Americans employ some type of complementary and alternative health practice or product, spending over $30 billion on treatments and preventions that often are not covered by traditional insurance. The American Wellness Network reports that the number of visits to complementary and alternative practitioners is double that of conventional practitioners.

As we shift to a wellness culture that empowers individuals to take responsibility for their own health, awareness is increasing that disease is not only preventable but reversible. As the total cost of healthcare and related expenses approaches 15 percent of our Gross National Product and we don't seem to be getting much healthier, some believe that the new wellness trend could actually reduce the percentage of dollars spent on health care over the next ten years instead of the anticipated increase of over 30 percent.

Many of the leading medical research centers are advocating the integration of energy practices in combination with traditional healthcare in treating individuals with life-threatening illnesses. Spiritual healers are even working alongside anesthesiologists in operating rooms to support the care of the "spiritual body" during major operations. "Alternative" therapies that were once considered useless and even dangerous quackery are now being taught in the clinics of major medical centers. Dr. David M. Eisenberg, author of *Encounters with Qi*, is heading up the Harvard Medical School's Division for Research and Education in Complementary and Integrative Medical Therapies, which was launched in the spring of 2000. HMS was recently awarded a grant of two million dollars from the National Institutes of Health to create the first model of integrative care within an academic teaching hospital.

Interest in these low-cost and non-invasive approaches has been led by consumers, pushing many in the medical professions into reluctant acceptance of the growing evidence of their effectiveness, evidence that is abundantly available in other countries where these treatments have long been a normal part of the healthcare system. This doesn't mean that modern technology has no place in today's eclectic approach to health, only that there needs to be more of a balance between medicine-as-usual and ancient healing traditions.

Many of the diagnostic systems already in use in conventional medicine are based on the principles of energy medicine. These include the electrocardiogram (EKG), which measures the activity of the heart; magnetic resonance imaging (MRI), which creates images of internal organs; and the electroencephalogram (EEG), which measures brain waves. In recent years a number of diagnostic systems have been developed to measure the strength of energy meridian frequencies. These machines provide an early warning system for physical imbalances so that we can see a disease coming before it manifests.

TAKING RESPONSIBILITY
FOR OUR HEALTH

In his book *Vital Energy: The Seven Keys to Invigorate Body, Mind, and Soul*, Dr. David Simon urges his readers to overcome inertia, look closely at the quality of their lives, and commit to a new way of living. "The obstacles to vitality," he writes, "exist on a subtler level. Emotional clarity, nourishing relationships, and meaningful work are needed to get [people's] juices flowing. They must reduce their tolerance for toxicity, be it toxic substances, emotions, or relationships, in order for vital energy to flow."

The idea of taking responsibility for your own health is not well-developed in this society. Dependent on and conditioned to accept the system we have, most of us don't categorize ourselves as healers or feel we have self-healing potential. We cede that role to the experts, however uncertain we may be of their skills. Such an attitude is a problem, for it has led us to treat our bodies like our automobiles: we take them in to get serviced. If a part breaks down, we wait in line for a replacement. In the story below, a woman's father remained loyal to the medical status quo even as his health continued to decline.

Linda's Story

Early one Sunday morning not long ago, I sat beside a dying man in a small hospital room, watching his tired face as he asked to be detached from the machine that had been his lungs for the past several days. He knew that his bout with respiratory illness was lost, but he wanted to take the last few breaths on his own. The man, determined in his final moments to leave this world feeling some small sense of victory, was my father.

For my dad, traditional medicine and those who practiced it were part of a system he accepted totally. This belief gave him a sense of peace that I did not share, knowing of the options—explored and otherwise—that he was unwilling to consider. My father was 86 when he died. "He had a long life," said his friends. "He had longevity," I would say, "but without vitality, who wants it?" My dad became ill in his sixties, and for the last 20 years of his life moved steadily from wellness to invalid.

Fortunately, such attitudes are changing as growing numbers of people—including Linda—explore and even embrace the energy practices of ancient traditions. Her story continues:

I can personally testify to the effectiveness of what Andrew Weil, M.D., calls "complementary medicine": a pre-cancerous condition in my body was detected, diagnosed, and treated without drugs, and successfully eliminated over a two-year period. The methods and mechanisms used for my healing process would have been harshly judged as "quackery" by my parents and many others.

This growing acceptance is no less evident among some of the doctors who are treating us. The role of primary care physicians has changed dramatically in the last decade, and we can expect even more changes in the future. Spirituality, healing, and medicine are coming together in creative new ways that are making some of today's doctors look like their ancient counterparts. "Through cross-cultural research into medicine men, shamans, and healers," writes Dr. David Simon in *Vital Energy*, "I came to the understanding that the traditional role of doctor was much more than that of a disease technician. The healer was a societally sanctioned explorer into the subtle aspects of the physical, emotional, and spiritual realms of life. The doctor had to be diagnostician, medicine man, psychotherapist, and priest. Disease was viewed as a lack of integration between body, mind, and spirit, and healing was the reintegration of these layers."

ENERGY MEDICINE: WHERE THE ANCIENT AND THE MODERN ARE INTERSECTING

Sickness or disease arise when the quality and strength of your personal energy deteriorates. Consequently, healing cannot occur—no matter by what name it is known—unless some kind of shift in energy takes place. Balance can only be reestablished when a strong flow of energy is restored and the body is realigned.

Western medicine has historically disregarded this approach to health and healing. It views illness as a mechanical breakdown and considers individuals with life-threatening disease as, at best, the victims of a sometimes dangerous world, and at worst as somehow the cause of their own suffering. Allopathic medicine is very good at treating injuries and accidents but generally ineffective for treating the whole person and his or her energy field—the only true source of healing. Radiation, chemotherapy, surgeries, and drugs can alleviate or even eliminate a serious problem, but the results are often temporary, and many who follow a prescribed treatment of drugs or chemotherapy and then go into remission are eventually re-diagnosed with the same illness.

Such an outcome would have made sense to the authors of *The Yellow Emperor's Classic of Internal Medicine* (circa 400 B.C.), in which they wrote "To administer medicine to diseases which have already developed and thereby suppress bodily chaos which has already occurred is comparable to the behavior of those who would begin to dig a well after they had grown thirsty, or those who would begin to cast weapons after they have engaged in battle. Would these actions not be too late?"

The Chinese would define a health crisis such as cancer as a serious case of stagnant chi, a message from the body that something is out of balance. They would then evaluate the flow of energy through a person's body and which areas of their external life may also be stagnant—their relationships, their work, where and how they live. Like many Western doctors, they would advocate such things as lifestyle and dietary changes, but they would also prescribe certain energy practices and engage the person directly in their own healing process. In short, rather than "fix" their patients, as those in the West would typically do, rather than suggest that the patient is bad or has done something wrong to have created such a condition, they would simply see the symptoms as important information, share the responsibility for healing, and seek long-term and systemic solutions.

POWER NOTES

- Leading medical research centers are advocating the integration of energy practices with traditional healthcare to treat individuals with life-threatening illness.
- "Alternative" therapies that were once considered useless and even dangerous quackery are now being taught in the clinics of major medical centers.
- Many of the diagnostic systems already in use in conventional medicine are based on the principles of energy medicine.
- Spirituality, healing and medicine are coming together in creative new ways that are making some of today's doctors look like their ancient counterparts.
- Sickness or disease arise when the quality and strength of your personal energy deteriorates.
- Balance can only be reestablished when a strong flow of energy is restored and the body is realigned.
- Like many Western doctors, the Chinese would advocate such things as lifestyle and dietary changes, but they would also prescribe specific energy practices and engage the person directly in the healing process.

CHAPTER THIRTEEN

Facilitating Wellness

Each of us is truly our primary doctor with nature as our guide.
We have all the healing knowledge we need within our very
beings. Learning to make contact with the healing ability
within and using this knowledge in our daily life is the route
to better and better health and well-being.

ELSON M. HAAS, M.D.,
Staying Healthy with the Seasons

Most of us can easily understand the need for personal healing when we've been diagnosed with a life-threatening illness, or even when we're just not feeling up to par. It's much more difficult for people to explore what might need healing when it comes to discomfort in their relationships, emotions, or attitudes. While numerous books, workshops, and seminars are designed to support individuals on their path toward greater self-awareness, only a courageous few are actually participating to a more than superficial extent.

Some people feel that to read a book on personal growth or attend a workshop on self-improvement means that they are admitting that there's something wrong with them. As someone who has read a great deal on human potential and participated in many seminars and workshops, I view my involvement differently. I believe that this brief time we have on earth is for the purpose of learning and growth. I'm not perfect, nor do I aspire to be.

But I do have an interest in attaining greater self-awareness, and in living a life of greater ease and grace.

As a student of ancient and indigenous cultures for most of my adult life, I am curious and often baffled why so few have embraced the powerful body of knowledge represented by these traditions. The energy and healing practices they relied (and still rely) on have the capacity not only to improve our physical, emotional, mental, and spiritual health and well-being, but to produce what we might term miraculous results in our physical bodies, our families, our relationships, and even our businesses.

ENERGY PRACTICES

Instruction in yoga, Tai Chi, feng shui, and meditation is now available in most major cities and towns. The basics are easy—even modest practice can provide great benefits—and most of them can be done by people of any age. While there are complex variations on these various methods, I'm not convinced that they produce any greater benefits. What is most important is that you incorporate a realistic, *daily* practice into your life; anything less will not achieve the results you want. A routine as modest as ten or fifteen minutes in the morning and ten or fifteen minutes in the early evening will start generating positive changes.

Energy disciplines, whether mentally or physically focused, allow us to become more relaxed and receptive. It then becomes easier to remove blockages in our bodies or minds. Addressing these blockages will lead to insights into problems, a lessening of stress, improved health and increased productivity. Chi Gung, meditation, yoga, and other such disciplines put the power back into your hands. Their preventive effects can help resolve the crises in our healthcare system and reduce the influence of the pharmaceutical industry on the over-medicated culture it has created.

The more we understand the concepts of energy and how we are affected in both positive and detrimental ways by its movement and quality, the easier it will be for us to change our environments, our relationships, and the health of our bodies. When you start to incorporate energy practices into your daily life, you will come to view what is sometimes called "miraculous healing" as logical and understandable and not some kind of mystery or magic. (You'll read more about "miracle healing" in the next chapter.)

EVERY JOURNEY BEGINS WITH A FIRST STEP

We were given a body and a heart and a mind when we came into this life, but no one gave us the operating instructions. We were encouraged to learn to read, to write, and to do math, yet we were never informed that we have the capacity to heal ourselves and fulfill our highest dreams and goals. But we can. And it's never too late to begin.

Once you've learned to view your life as energy, dramatic changes will occur in how you treat your body, perceive human relationships, and overcome challenges. When you can achieve and maintain a state of heightened energy in all four areas of intelligence, you will have taken the important first steps in regaining control of your life. You won't back down from the problems and obstacles. You'll know almost immediately when your body and your spirit are out of balance and then take appropriate actions to realign them. Your immune system will automatically operate more effectively.

The confidence that come from having a finely tuned energy body and fully developed intelligences also enables you to contribute to the health and well-being of others. When you can bring your full awareness into the work you do and your interactions with the people you meet each day—no matter their age, status, or interests—you will have learned the art of achieving personal power.

When you begin to achieve this personal mastery, you lose the need to control every aspect of your life and the individuals around you. When you go beyond your conscious intelligence and develop the skills of inner knowing, you will intuitively know what is right for you, whether it's a personal investment, the right doctor, vitamin supplements or medications, the correct fitness program, the foods you should eat and the ones you shouldn't, which career or business opportunities to pursue, and which people and relationships will nurture you.

THE KEYS TO OPTIMAL HEALTH

With the media telling us what to think and believe and how to live, it's no wonder that millions of us are looking for an escape, often into the numbing distraction of addictive behaviors. And yet our lives don't need to be plagued by relentless challenges, obstacles, and crises. I'm not suggesting that we shield ourselves from our own personal problems or the world's social and economic injustices, but we do have the power to live a full, rewarding, and productive life despite the turmoil around us.

It begins with getting clear about what truly fills you with energy, passion, and purpose, because every day that you're not living your passion or fulfilling your dreams, you're accelerating the aging process and shortening your life span. I keep going back to the question asked by Seneca elders when contemplating the wisdom of a particular action: *Am I contributing to a greater degree of harmony in myself and the world with this action, or adding to the chaos and confusion?*

To create personal and business environments that are supportive, productive, and profitable, you need to understand how powerful you truly are. You also need simple practices and principles that become part of your basic nature and understanding. The following are principles that have worked for me:

- Learn how to tell the truth—both to yourself and others—about what you truly value.
- Identify what you're truly committed to and declare that you're no longer willing to waste your vitality and energy on anything else.
- Prioritize your intentions and create an action plan to set your life going in a new direction.

- Work to release attitudes that produce anger, disappointment, fear, sadness, and feelings of loss.
- Choose activities that create a positive emotional charge and feelings of excitement, joy, pleasure, and passion.
- Avoid toxic relationships or being around people who drain your energy.
- Look at individuals who cause you tension and stress as helping you move toward a higher level of consciousness. People aren't the problem, only your perceptions of them.
- Engage in activities that make you feel valued and worthy, such as volunteering at your church, local senior center, or a listener-supported radio station.

On a more physical level, doctors and wellness experts agree that to maintain a healthy body, mind and spirit, individuals should follow a daily regimen that includes some or all of the following:

- Practice some kind of stress-reducing technique (meditation, deep breathing, yoga, Chi Gung, toning).
- Spend at least one hour a day outdoors.
- Choose work that you enjoy and that gives you a sense of purpose and contribution.
- Surround yourself with people you feel comfortable with and who also contribute to your personal growth.
- When possible, consume foods and beverages that are free from pesticides, chemicals, and genetic manipulation. This will help prevent serious health problems, improve your ability to operate at peak performance, and benefit the earth by supporting healthy farming techniques.
- Express gratitude every day for the opportunities and blessings you do have.

SHIFTING TO BALANCE

In the final analysis, health and a sense of well-being are
perhaps the most important factors in life and everyone
needs the opportunity to have access to modern technology
as well as understanding something of the ancient traditions
of healing.

The Encyclopedia of Alternative Medicine

In learning the basics of energy practice and management, you will have begun the important process of shifting your body from burnout to balance
and creating more harmony in your home, at work, in your relationships,
and in your community. Another important benefit is that the more we explore cultures other than our own, the more likely we'll learn to appreciate
the wisdom of their beliefs and therapeutic practices, and the more kinship
and respect we will feel on a human level.

A skilled practitioner can certainly help someone through a difficult
healing crisis or with a temporary discomfort or imbalance, but permanent
recovery and spiritual growth ultimately require the ability to self-heal. It's
my belief that when we more consciously understand and take care of our
physical bodies, we'll also take better care of our lives and our planet. We all
have the capacity to heal ourselves, our relationships, our businesses and
communities, and the Earth that we depend on for sustenance. We just need
to remember what we already know.

POWER NOTES

- The more you understand the concepts of energy and how you are affected in both positive and detrimental ways by its movement and quality, the easier it will be for you to change your environments, your relationships, and the health of your body.

- When you start to incorporate energy practices into your daily life, you will come to view what is sometimes called "miraculous healing" as logical and understandable and not some kind of mystery or magic.

- Once you've learned to view your life as energy, dramatic changes will occur in how you treat your body, perceive human relationships, and overcome challenges.

- The confidence that comes from having a finely tuned energy body and fully developed intelligences will also enable you to contribute to the health and well-being of others.

- Every day that you're not living your passion or fulfilling your dreams, you're accelerating the aging process and shortening your life span.

- We all have the capacity to heal ourselves, our relationships, our businesses and communities, and the Earth that we depend on for sustenance. We just need to remember what we already know.

BELIEVE IN MIRACLES

CHAPTER FOURTEEN

Everyday Miracles

> This . . .is about bringing our light back into proper circulation. . . . Incomplete circulation in our bodies forms patterns. These patterns predispose our bodies to diseases, which can shorten our life span. Disease patterns are like cobwebs that develop when the web of light around the body is not energized in its completeness. It is similar to the cobwebs that gather in a corner of a building due to lack of circulation.
>
> DANIEL SANTOS,
Luminous Essence

"Light"—its brightness, its color—is commonly associated with the concepts of healing and energy; in many religious beliefs light represents divine power. At an energetic level, our cells emit bright light when we're healthy and darken when we're stressed. Think about some of the people you know. Those who radiate optimism and goodwill almost seem filled with light; those who seem troubled or withdrawn will have a completely different "feel" to them, and often that feeling is dark.

In *Luminous Essence*, Daniel Santos synthesizes Eastern teachings (from both India and China), ancient shamanistic medicine and the Native American cosmologies of North America, South America, and Mexico with Western science and medicine in discussing the dynamics of energy and light. Santos states:

We can only feel whole and complete when we embody our potential. To do this we must understand both personal and cultural patterns of ill health and how our negative experiences of life are stored in areas of our bodies. We must also understand the manner in which diseases are culturally transmitted through generations.

ENERGY HEALING

Alberto Villoldo is a classically trained medical anthropologist who has studied the shamanic healing techniques of the ancient Incas for more than twenty years. The author of numerous books, he teaches energy medicine to thousands of medical professionals and laypeople every year. In *Shaman, Healer, Sage,* he explains that central to the practice of shamanic (some might say "miraculous") healing is the concept of the Luminous Energy Field, believed to surround our material bodies. He compares this belief to the practice of yoga, which in Sanskrit means "yoking": uniting that which has been separated. The basic foundation of yoga is thus to unite the mundane with the divine in order to become whole. Shamans, on the other hand, assume that an inherent unity always exists within each person and they work within that framework.

Villoldo believes that while psychological healing can release disruptive emotional energy that has been trapped, such healing often lasts for just a short period of time. Trying to understand a trauma intellectually, with our mental intelligence alone, simply doesn't go deep enough into the damage. Psychological issues are thus likely to return, and some individuals continue with talk therapy for years. That is why shamans and those who've learned from their traditions try to effect change at a deeper, more structural level—at the level of the energy body.

THE WONDERS OF REIKI

The Reiki techniques of energy work were founded by Dr. Mikao Usui in the 1880s. Reiki, polarity, and other hands-on healing therapies that work directly with energy are designed to accomplish what Santos refers to above: eliminating the cobwebs. Reiki is a Japanese word that translates as "universal spirit," "universal life energy," or "God light energy." Reiki masters believe that this all-pervading benevolent energy can override negativity and bring health and vitality to body, mind, and spirit, and they consider themselves conduits of this energy. Practitioners also believe that people are born with the ability to access healing light energy, but that over time we lose this ability as our energetic systems become blocked. Removing these blocks is done through the laying of hands on specific areas of the body. Practitioners read the subtle energy fields of a recipient and then use that knowledge to work out energetic knots, bypassing emotional and mental complications that reside closer to the surface.

While shamanic work varies with each culture and practitioner, Reiki, polarity, and therapeutic touch rely on specific structures and systems. At the same time, all of these approaches are non-invasive, provide useful tools for self-awareness and transformation, and are based on a system of healing using spiritually guided life force energy. They are most often experienced with a practitioner, but the techniques, including the use of "internal scanning" (a method of using our own abilities of concentration and visualization to detect problems), can be learned for self-treatment.

Two books that describe Reiki in more depth are *Practical Reiki* by Richard Ellis and *The Book of Ch'i* by Paul Wildish. Both are amply illustrated and easy to understand; both relate the fascinating story of the search that took Dr. Usui from his position as dean of a Christian theological seminary to a Zen monastery in Kyoto, Japan, to more deeply penetrate the secrets of healing power. In his quest for spiritual healing, Dr. Usui discovered Five Spiritual Principles of healing that form the basis of Reiki:

1. Just for today, let go of anger.
2. Just for today, let go of worry.
3. Just for today, count your blessings and honor your parents, teachers, and neighbors.
4. Just for today, live honestly.
5. Just for today, be kind to all living things.

Reiki's most immediate benefit is tension reduction and the release of contracted muscles. It has also proven effective in comforting patients with anxieties and fears, particularly the terminally ill. Its ability to provide a feeling of peace and serenity has played a vital role in supporting those who are dealing with life-threatening conditions.

One of the practices described in the book *Practical Reiki* by Richard Ellis is called "Internal Scanning," which engages our abilities of concentration and visualization. I describe it as the use of awareness to identify or detect areas in the body that are either currently experiencing disease or are susceptible to disease. I believe that human beings truly possess the intelligence to diagnose and heal their own illnesses—this is our divine heritage—and that such tools as internal scanning can help us do this.

There are skeptics, of course, but such hands-on therapies are increasingly being used in hospitals across the U.S., and for good reason. A recent series of clinical trials carried out at the University of Maryland School of Medicine's Complementary Medicine Program, for example, found that of the eleven studies involving therapeutic touch, seven showed at least one positive treatment effect. Remember, this is all energy work—no drugs, no needles, no surgery, no doctor visits.

INITIATIONS

I was first introduced to Reiki through my participation in Gay Luce's Nine Gates Mystery School, where I received the initiation of the First Degree (the first of three). After returning and completing the Mystery School,

I sought out a local practitioner, Pam Adler, with whom I repeated the First Degree and received the Second Degree initiation. I haven't yet completed my Reiki Master training because my primary interest has been to use if for myself and for friends and family members. I have found it very effective in eliminating stress and boosting energy. It really came in handy while I was trekking in the Annapurna range of Nepal several years ago.

My intention to take such a rigorous hike was to motivate myself to get into better shape. Between one thing and another, not least of things a demanding work schedule, I never quite got around to doing the necessary preparation. I was also having trouble with my knees—the usual aches of middle age. And yet off I went anyway, as planned. Luckily I didn't have weather to contend with; it was beautiful and mild. Of course I knew that we would be hiking uphill, at least to start, but I had no real idea what I was getting myself into.

I would liken our average daily trek to walking up and down stadium steps for five to seven hours straight, although we did take a short lunch break. Every night I would practice Reiki on my legs—a simple resting of my hands on my knees. After the first day, when reality set in as to what was in store, I was a little nervous about how I would feel the next day. To my amazement, when I woke up early the next morning, I had no experience of pain or tightness. In the days that followed, my legs continued to respond to my touch, and what might have been hours of torture turned out to be blessedly without incident.

EVERYDAY MIRACLES

In 1995, Luke Chan spent a month at the Huazia Ahineng Qigong Clinic and Training Center—known simply as The Center—to find out what was going on in this medicine-less hospital. Established in 1988 in Qinhuangdao, five hours by train from Beijing. The Center was founded by Dr. Pang Ming, a physician and qigong grand master trained in both Western and Chinese traditional medicine. The Center does not promote special diets and avoids the use of medicines. What The Center does offer and specialize in is exercise, love, and restoring chi, based on a variation of Chi Gung that Ming calls Chi Lel.

By the end of his stay, Chan was convinced that something special was happening at this otherwise nondescript clinic. In the foreword to his book *101 Miracles of Natural Healing*, he writes:

> I was stunned when I videotaped the ultrasound image of a cancerous tumor as it was being "removed' naturally, under the supervision of doctors, by Chi Lel teachers in China. I immediately felt that the self-healing art of Chi Lel must be a new frontier in fighting disease, which everyone should know about.
>
> Upon returning to the United States, I told many people about it, but most of them were skeptical, saying "I haven't seen it on TV." So I called all the TV stations in my local area to tell them the good news. Only one reporter expressed any interest, and she stipulated that only if I had a doctor to comment on the footage would she consider looking at it. I called a number of doctors but none were interested.

Chan's book goes on to tell the truly amazing and heart-warming stories of 101 individuals who were faced with life-threatening illnesses and cured themselves while at The Center. The Center has indeed produced some remarkable results: a more than 95-percent success rate of healing in their patients! One of the keys to its success is that those in the program are referred to as students, never patients. The rationale is that the people who come to The Center are learning an art whose ultimate goal is healing themselves.

When Chan asked the founder why he didn't promote Chi Lel to the world sooner, Dr. Pang Ming replied that many people need proof that a practice works. So instead of arguing, he worked slowly, collecting tens of thousands of documented cases over a period of eight years.

I understand Mr. Chan's frustration at being aware of so many types of cures founded on the practices of the ancients—cures that are creating what we might call miracles—that have still not been accepted by mainstream medicine. What many view as miraculous—such as unexplained healing—is just a shift in reality or perception. This understanding is the key to the ability of shamans and true healers to bring about remarkable changes.

POWER NOTES

- "Light"—its brightness, its color—is commonly associated with the concepts of healing and energy; in many religious beliefs light represents divine power.
- Those who radiate optimism and goodwill almost seem filled with light; those who always seem troubled or withdrawn will have a completely different "feel" to them, and often that feeling is dark.
- While psychological healing can release disruptive emotional energy that has been trapped, such healing often lasts for just a short period of time.
- People are born with the ability to access healing light energy, but over time we lose this ability as our energetic systems become blocked.
- What many view as miraculous—such as unexplained healing—is just a shift in reality or perception.

CHAPTER FIFTEEN

Belief in a Greater Power

The beauty of prayer is that it is not necessary to know
precisely how it works to benefit from its miraculous effects.
In this universal technology, we are simply invited to experience, feel, and acknowledge what our feelings are saying to
us. Our prayers come to life as we focus upon the feeling
of our heart's desire, rather than the thought of our
knowing world.

GREGG BRADEN,
*The Isaiah Effect: Decoding the
Lost Science of Prayer and Prophecy*

Gregg Braden, a former computer systems designer and earth science expert, is the author of several books that provide fresh insight into the relationship between thoughts, feelings,
emotions, and what he describes as the lost science of prayer. Braden's in
sights are based on his extensive research into the Dead Sea Scrolls and the
work of the Essenes, a community of scholars (both male and female) that,
five hundred years before the birth of Christ, were vigorously studying a
variety of ancient teachings in their quest for ultimate spiritual knowledge.

It is believed that almost all of the principle founders of what would
later be called Christianity—St. Ann, Joseph and Mary, John the Baptist,
John the Evangelist, and, of course, Jesus—were Essenes. Their beliefs
about the nature of God and the universe are thought to have become part

of "nearly every major world belief system existing today including those of China, Tibet, Egypt, India, Palestine, Greece, and the American Southwest," writes Braden. Some of the traditions of the Freemasons, Gnostics, and Kabbalists also have their roots in this ancient lineage of wisdom.

The worldview of the Essenes was founded on the belief that the relationship between our bodies and our feelings is directly intertwined with the elements of the earth, and that humans represent the union of the masculine force of "our Father in Heaven" and the feminine power of "our Mother Earth." The Essenes also asserted that our thoughts, feelings, and emotions—our inner world—mirrored the larger reality of our families and communities—our outer world—and vice versa. Consequently, when our collective inner worlds are dominated by fear, anger, and confusion, the outer world looks much the same, and you end up with oppression, deceit, warfare, disease, and the many other ravages that plague this planet.

When you respond to life events and situations as if they were outside of your body and your control, then you'll perceive the solutions as being out of your control as well. For example, if you think of the body as mechanical and disease as something that originates somewhere else, then you'll focus only on externally generated solutions. On the other hand, if you view your body as sacred, certain that you have some control over how it works, then when something "goes wrong" you'll be more likely to look inside for solutions, thus connecting with a deeper source of healing and power.

THE MANY WAYS TO PRAY

Reconciling these two worlds, the inner and the outer, is one of the primary purposes of prayer. It is a way of acknowledging the connection between humans and the divine through our conscious intention to do good, to serve others, and to improve ourselves. Sometimes we pray in gratitude, giving thanks for all that we have been given. Sometimes our prayers are like a petition, when we have a specific objective in mind. Shamanic cultures often use songs as prayer. I've heard others say that their yoga practice is a form of prayer. Feng shui and the practice of creating sacred space can also be prayer—a way to call in support and guidance and infuse our space with love and divine light.

Angeles Arrien recalls the distinction made by a nine-year-old child on the difference between prayer and meditation: "Prayer is when you talk to God," the little girl explained, "and meditation is when you listen to what God has to say."

EXPRESSING GRATITUDE

The practice of gratitude assumes that we have faith that something greater than ourselves is providing guidance and protection. It is also one of the primary means of using energy to turn desires into reality. Ironically, the key is to focus on being thankful for what we have, not on what we don't have. This is difficult to do when we are besieged by the demands of a materialistic society. And yet worrying about what is missing from our lives simply reinforces our belief (and our fear) that what we want is difficult to obtain, and that what we don't have means a less than perfect life.

Expressing your gratitude daily for what you have (instead of worrying about what you want and don't have) is an especially powerful form of prayer. As a form of prayer, gratitude can increase your energy frequencies to a high enough vibratory level to eliminate tension and even fight disease. As you express gratitude, you can more readily access states of compassion and love and feel a greater connection to and awareness of the Oneness of everything in the universe.

As motivational consultant Anthony Robbins said, "I believe the ultimate path to enlightenment is the cultivation of gratitude. When you're grateful, fear disappears. When you're grateful, lack disappears. When you're grateful, self-significance disappears. You feel a sense that your life is uniquely blessed, but at the same time you feel like you're a part of everything that exists and you know that you are not the source of it. In that state you show up differently for the people around you. Just walking around, you vibrate."

THE POWER OF PRAYER TO HEAL

Larry Dossey is author of numerous books (*Prayer Is Good Medicine; Healing Words; and Reinventing Medicine, among others*), executive editor of the peer-review journal *Alternative Therapies in Health and Medicine*, and recipient along with his wife Barbara of the first annual Pioneer of Integrative Medicine Award. He is one of the most respected physicians in the field of body-mind health. A former chief of staff at Humana Medical City Dallas Hospital, he speaks with authority on the evolution of medicine and the increasing role that energy and even prayer are playing in it.

The impact of prayer on healing is a recent and quite controversial topic, and Dossey, an advocate, admits that the challenges are significant in proving its efficacy. Part of the problem, says Dossey, is that there are no scientific theories that can explain *how* prayer heals. And despite numerous studies performed in the last fifteen years, irrefutable evidence has yet to be established.

At the same time, positive outcomes have been documented, including a study of heart attack victims in 1988 and Elizabeth Targ's 1998 study of AIDS patients at the Pacific College of Medicine in San Francisco, which found a strong correlation between intercessory prayer and the length of a hospital stay. New studies are under way at Duke University Medical Center, the University of Washington, and other noted colleges around the country.

Whether or not the healing power of prayer is an accepted reality, it's more helpful to remember that prayer itself heals in subtle ways that don't necessarily show up in a medical report. "We continually need to examine what we think prayer is 'for,'" says Dossey. "Is it a way of getting things? Think of the Big Three things most people are striving for—health and longevity, prosperity and fulfilling relationships. We can pray to be blessed with such things; it's our nature to do so. But these are minor compared with the larger lessons of prayer—which is to reveal to us that we're already divine, eternal, and immortal."

Michelle's Story

In 1996 I was diagnosed with cervical cancer. I had just turned 28. I have two beautiful girls who, at the time, were only six months and four years old. After being treated with a radical hysterectomy, I was told I had a 99.9% chance that my cancer would not return. But in December of 2000, I found a lump in my collarbone area. The doctor found numerous tumors throughout my lymphatic system. I was given a 25% chance of lasting another five years. I thought, 'In five years I will still consider myself a newlywed, and my children will be just 12 and 9.' That was unacceptable to me, and I determined to figure out a way to survive. So I prayed...and prayed and prayed.

When we came to the Cancer Care Center, things weren't looking so good. We had already been through a number of unbelievable battles with an HMO and the doctors that are bound by them. Like fighting cancer isn't enough, huh?

On a Saturday night just before we started radiation (at this point I had just received my second dose of chemotherapy), I wasn't feeling well and was praying for a ray of hope when my husband came to my bedside with our girls and together we prayed for my recovery. They asked God for mercy and grace, and to heal me.

After my husband put the kids to bed, I was prompted to feel the lump in my neck again. I sat up and checked, and the lump was gone! It was there the day before. It did not shrink or move. It was totally gone! Since the plan was to shrink the tumors with radiation and I hadn't even started it yet, well, was this the ray of hope we had prayed for? In the Bible God says He will never leave you nor forsake you. I felt that He was showing me that He was still there with me.

Prayer works, whether you are praying to God, a goddess, Buddha, Allah, the Great Spirit, or just spinning a Tibetan prayer wheel. As Joseph Campbell once said: "The Bible says the kingdom of heaven is within. Who's in heaven? God! So God is within!"

THE POWER OF THOUGHTS

The body is the servant of the mind. It obeys the operations of the mind, whether they be deliberately chosen or automatically expressed. At the bidding of unlawful thoughts the body sinks rapidly into disease and decay; at the command of glad and beautiful thoughts it becomes clothed with youthfulness and beauty. Disease and health, like circumstances, are rooted in thought. . . . Thoughts of fear have been known to kill a man as speedily as a bullet, and they are continually killing thousands of people just as surely though less rapidly. The people who live in fear of disease are the people who get it.

JAMES ALLEN,
As a Man Thinketh

Indigenous cultures understand that a human being's thoughts, intentions, and dreams don't just influence but also control that person's health and quality of life. Every time we have a thought, whether it is positive or negative, we have started—or kept—a ball rolling in one direction or another. Repeated negative thoughts about how difficult work is, for example, will keep you in a "work is bad" state of mind, squeezing out possibilities for change. Holding a positive outlook, on the other hand, will help to create the conditions for achieving whatever goal you're pursuing.

Unfortunately, Western cultures have had little training in how to change undesirable conditions into more desirable ones using the power of thought control and the knowledge of how energy works. We are aware enough to know that when we exert too much physical energy we become tired and drained. We notice as well that certain activities deplete us more than others, whether it's a trip to the shopping mall or a lengthy business meeting.

Much of the time, though, our thoughts, feelings, and emotions are out of sync with each other, and imbalance occurs. For example, we may *want* more abundance, but if we carry a deep belief that we don't really deserve it, then it will be difficult to manifest that reality. Negative emotions and mindsets such as anger, guilt, shame, unworthiness, low self-esteem, or resentment prevent us from moving toward more positive outcomes in life. If we want to change our work, our lives, and ultimately our world, we need to change what we spend our energy thinking about.

When we can achieve more mental and emotional balance, we create the conditions for a greater degree of wisdom and self-confidence. The good news is that, at any time, we can turn our thoughts and inner images in a more life-affirming direction and release the ones that no longer serve us, that perpetuate cycles of negativity and disease.

> Winning this game of life requires power and energy. The sources of power and energy seldom come from a glamorous façade but rather from the hidden treasures that are often forgotten or overlooked. According to shamanic lore, without the power and energy to win, you will lose the game or be left in the dust while others survive and succeed. . . . When we truly realize the power of our words to create and make things happen, we can never again feel a victim of life or even choose to use words in foolish ways.
>
> JOSE STEVENS, PH.D., with LENA STEVENS:
> *The Power Path: The Shaman's Way*
> *to Success in Business and Life*

AMAZING TRANSFORMATIONS
VIA THOUGHTS

Japanese visionary and researcher Masaru Emoto is conducting some interesting research on the power of thought, as revealed in the popular movie *What the Bleep Do We Know?* and in his book *The Hidden Messages in Water.* In the book, Emoto relates how he and his colleagues conducted numerous experiments by taping various words and phrases to a glass jar filled with water. They let the water stand overnight, froze it the next day, and then photographed the frozen crystal formations under an electron microscope. The process showed that in polluted and toxic water, the crystal structures were distorted. But the crystals in the water that had taped to it the words "love and appreciation" were lacy and beautiful, like a snowflake. Further, when the words "You make me sick. I will kill you" were taped onto a jar, the crystallized pattern was clearly deformed.

Emoto also photographed water that was exposed to different types of music. The crystalline structure of water exposed to a Tibetan sutra, for example, was discernibly more symmetrical and elegant than that of water that "heard" heavy metal music. His experiments suggest that water is highly responsive to our thoughts and emotions, and takes on the vibrations and energy of its environment. And isn't the human body almost 90% water? Emoto concludes that we can positively heal and transform our planet and ourselves by the thoughts we think, as well as the ones we put into action.

At the third annual conference of The International Society for the Study of Subtle Energies and Energy Medicine (ISSSEEM), numerous studies revealed that when individuals focused on feelings of deep love, "they were able to intentionally cause a change in the conformation (shape) of the DNA." An astounding finding! It suggests that emotion may provide a direct line of communication to our cellular functions and even to the very core of life, and that we have control over that force. How wisely will we use it? Gregg Braden states that the ancient texts he has studied speak of a certainty that our successes and failures are opportunities to know more of ourselves and to develop mastery. Every event in our lives, from work to relationships to family struggles, every emotion we feel and action we take, draw us either closer to or further away from this mastery. Through prayer, compassion, gratitude, and love, by understanding the laws of cause and effect and taking decisive positive actions, we can pass those tests and experience our potential as human beings.

MANIFESTING THE LIFE YOU DESIRE

Successful people appear to manifest what they want in life with very little effort. And because it seems effortless, we believe it's the result of long hours, advanced degrees, or a high level of mental intelligence. Success, power, and the ability to manifest ultimately do not originate from such efforts or talents, though; they fall into the category of otherworldly, as they cannot truly be explained with any degree of accuracy or depth by the measures of a material world.

The real key is maintaining internal balance, drawing from the principles of energy and the power of thought to change reality as discussed throughout this book. The workbook in Part Two offers additional support in achieving this inner state of stability.

The extent to which you can achieve such a balance is the extent to which you will control the events in your life. Every time you take the time to observe and evaluate your reactions, feelings, or responses in a challenging situation, you accelerate your growth on the path of mastery. The more observant and conscious you become, the more you increase and expand your energy. When you begin to do this consistently, you will start to attract the right opportunities and people. And when you accept others, understanding that they are exactly where they need to be in their life work and process, you further energize your own growth.

If you perceive that everything in the world is interconnected, then all actions you take on behalf of your own spiritual growth will benefit all of mankind. The speeding up of the world that we have all noted and struggled with also means that the dynamics of cause and effect—the maxim that every action creates an equal and opposite reaction—have also accelerated. The result: it's getting easier and easier to manifest what you want in life when you use the right tools, while the impacts of wrongful actions are also more readily evident.

When you learn how to slow down, simplify your life, and create an environment that nourishes your spirit, your life will be more balanced, harmonious, and fulfilling. When you become more centered, focused, and balanced, you can make wise decisions. You'll then be able to discover the nature of your own particular genius, stop trying to conform to other people's models, and learn to be your authentic, individuated self.

POWER NOTES

- When you respond to life events and situations as if they were outside of your body and your control, then you'll perceive the solutions as being out of your control as well.
- Expressing your gratitude daily for what you have (instead of worrying about what you want and don't have) is an especially powerful form of prayer.
- If you view your body as sacred, certain that you have some control over how it works, then when something "goes wrong" you'll be more likely to look inside for solutions, thus connecting with a deeper source of healing and power.
- Gratitude can increase your energy frequencies to a high enough vibratory level to eliminate tension and even fight disease.
- It's helpful to remember that prayer itself heals in subtle ways that don't necessarily show up in a medical report.
- Prayer works whether you are praying to God, a goddess, Buddha, Allah, or Great Spirit, or just spinning a Tibetan prayer wheel.
- If we want to change our work, our lives, and ultimately our world, we need to change what we spend our energy thinking about.
- The more observant and conscious you become, the more you increase and expand your energy.
- If you perceive that everything in the world is interconnected, then all actions you take on behalf of your own spiritual growth will benefit all of mankind.
- When you become more centered, focused, and balanced, you can make wise decisions.

PART TWO

MANIFEST YOUR DESIRES

A Guided Self-Inquiry and Action Plan

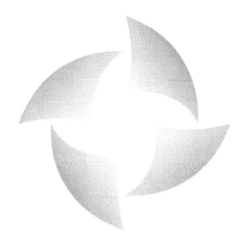

These pages are designed to help you examine your life and the choices you've made, and to rediscover the dreams and passions that are at the core of your life work and personal power. The exercises are intuitively ordered, moving from self-inquiry and remembering toward the creation of a plan to manifest the life you want to live.

The following section is intended as a "workbook" to help you reach your goals. Please photocopy the pages as needed, and use them to help focus your efforts.

The Value of Reflection

It is not a guiding spirit that reveals to me secretly in a flash
what I must say or do, but thought and reflection.

NAPOLEON (1769–1821)

We all have the capacity to re-make our lives in ways that help
us achieve our dreams. Like a story, we are each a unique
work of art. And like a story that isn't finished, we have the
power to change it.

Self-reflection and personal inquiry can help you to begin changing
your story, to see opportunities and life situations in a new light, and to discover new ideas and new wisdom.

Through reflection and personal inquiry, you can:

- Achieve greater life balance
- Identify the life work that nourishes your spirit
- Make positive changes in your personal and/or business life
- Clarify your unique genius, skills, and qualities
- Live a life of greater ease, confidence, and grace
- Implement the actions that will move you closer to your dreams

Use these exercises thoughtfully, answer honestly, and trust the process.
You have nothing to lose and everything to gain!

RE-ENVISION YOUR LIFE

> Ordinary people believe only in the possible. Extraordinary
> people visualize not what is possible or probable, but
> rather what is impossible. And by visualizing the impossible,
> they begin to see it as possible.
>
> CHERIE CARTER-SCOTT

Eeryone has the capacity to envision a better future for themselves, and then to design the actions and take the steps to manifest that reality. To begin this process, answer the following questions fully and carefully:

- What courses, classes, or workshops have you taken to identify your personal goals, vision, qualities, and purpose?
- What spiritual practices have you embraced or participated in?
- Which of them do you practice on a daily basis?
- What books have been the most valuable in assisting you with your personal growth?
- Do you keep a journal? If yes, how often do you write in it? Has it helped you?
- If not, what has kept you from doing so?

ARE YOU READY FOR A BREAKTHROUGH?

When I am anxious, it is because I am living in the future.
When I am depressed, it is because I am living in the past.
ANON.

When we're on the verge of a breakthrough regarding an important solution or new perspective, we can become more critical, more irritable, and less tolerant of others—family, friends, or co-workers. We also start noticing our impatience about events occurring in our personal or professional lives. We even become irritated about what's going on in our community or in world events as they are reported in the media.

Over the years, I've gradually learned to recognize these signs as positive messages. And so instead of trying to ignore them, or pretending to have a positive attitude, I use these times to really pay attention. I take more walks, spend more time in reflection, and make sure I'm rested.

Whether or not you find yourself in such a mental space, the following questions will help you move closer to discovering where you are and where you want to be.

- If you had more free time, how would you spend that time?
- How do you want to be remembered?
- Is your life in balance?
- What are you moving towards?
- What are you moving away from?
- Do you have clarity and focus about your direction?
- Are you always focused on doing as opposed to being?

WHAT IMPEDIMENTS PREVENT YOU FROM HAVING THE LIFE YOU WANT?

The ultimate of being successful is the luxury of giving yourself the time to do what you want to do.

LEONTYNE PRICE

In moving forward, it's valuable to reflect on what you see as the impediments that have prevented you from creating the life you desire. The following questions will help you identify the challenges and blocks that need to be dealt with in order to live the life you desire:

- What is the biggest challenge you are facing right now?
- Where have you stopped contributing?
- What conversations are louder than your commitments?
- What do you need to let go of to move forward (relationships, commitments, obligations, activities?
- What prevents you from manifesting your life dream or vision?

UNCOVERING THE PAST

*You have to count on living every single day in a way you
believe will make you feel good about your life, so that
if it were over tomorrow, you'd be content.*

JANE SEYMOUR

Your past holds many keys to your present. Some time spent reflecting on it
will help you understand its influence, and with understanding will come
the strength to make changes.

- What was the most challenging event from your past?
- Do you recall a significant and/or unpleasant event that occurred
  when you were between the ages of four and five?
- What were the circumstances, in your childhood or in the recent past,
  when you gave up your power?
- What do you not want people to know about you?
- What past actions have you taken that you are embarrassed or
  ashamed to tell anyone?
- Which of your personality traits has caused things to not work out?
- What did you once love to do but have stopped doing?
- What secret dreams have you given up on?

RECOVER YOUR DREAMS

> If we have not achieved our early dreams, we must either
> find new ones or see what we can salvage from the old. If
> we have accomplished what we set out to do in our youth,
> we need not weep like Alexander the Great that we have
> no more worlds to conquer.
>
> Rosalyn Carter

As children, most of us dreamed about what we would do when we grew up. These dreams changed daily and often, depending on our activities and exposure to new possibilities. But as we grew older, we experienced pressure to perform to our highest level—at school, in sports, at our hobbies—or to outperform others. Plans for the future became enmeshed with whether others liked us or how we would earn a living. The hobbies we chose often had more to do with what we "ought" to do than what we truly wanted to do.

The result: Most of our dreams became a distant or even forgotten memory. It's true that at a certain stage in life the desire to be an astronaut becomes unrealistic. But if you aren't feeling fulfilled in your career, there may be value in exploring what first caused you to fantasize about that spaceship. Maybe you're an adventurer at heart, or you like to discover new realities. It's never too late to remember the fantasies and visions that filled you with excitement, and then to draw on those to dream new dreams.

- What was your life like when you were ten?
- What did you love to do?
- What did you tell people you were going to be in the future?
- What did you feel deeply about?
- What traits in others annoyed you?
- What stories do you tell about your childhood or your past?
- Are there dreams or plans that you haven't fulfilled?

WHAT IS YOUR LIFE DREAM?

It is in our idleness, in our dreams, that the submerged truth
sometimes comes to the top.

VIRGINIA WOLF

Dare to dream big. Raise your expectations. Find a dream that inspires you.
If you can visualize it, it can become a reality.

- What are you here to learn?
- What are you here to teach?
- What fills you with joy?
- What's important to you?
- Who will support you (i.e., friends, partners, mentors, ancestors)?

IDENTIFY YOUR PERSONAL GENIUS

Thousands of geniuses live and die undiscovered—either
by themselves or by others.

MARK TWAIN

All of us want to contribute to something greater than ourselves, but doing
so can seem beyond reach. We may either downplay our abilities or assume
that what we can offer is much less than what is required to make a meaningful difference. In truth, the biggest contribution you can make to society
is to bring your unique qualities and skills to your life.

Skills and Qualities

- What are your unique skills and talents? What are you good at?
- What do colleagues, friends, and family most frequently acknowledge
  you for?
- What qualities would you like to receive greater acknowledgement
  for? What are your "secret" contributions?

What You Know

- People are always telling me that I'm _____.

- I get a lot of compliments about _____

- People often thank me for _____

- I am often acknowledged for being _____ .

- Deep in my soul, I know I am great at _____

WHAT DO YOU REALLY WANT?

It is only by following your deepest instinct that you can lead
a rich life, and if you let your fear of consequence prevent
you from following your deepest instinct, then your life will
be safe, expedient, and thin.

KATHERINE HATHAWAY

Those who manifest their goals easily project a certain quality of energy and
presence. For example, I've known many people who embody what I call
"the energy of money," attracting individuals and opportunities that help
them create abundance in their lives. And yet living a life of abundance has
little to do with your background or education. It has everything to do with
your intentions and your ability to focus on your goals. It also helps to
write them down and track them. If your goals and intentions aren't in
writing, it's more difficult to manifest what you want.

Before you begin the process of deciding what you really want in life,
consider how the following reflect—and in turn have influenced—the
choices you've made so far and the directions you've taken:

- Where you live
- Where you work
- Your most significant relationship
- Your hobbies, interests, and creative endeavors
- How you spend your free time
- Your political, religious, and spiritual beliefs and truths

Now think about the life you want to live. In designing this new future,
what changes would you make in the areas listed above? How about in
other areas?

WHAT IS YOUR PASSION AND PURPOSE?

When you're in your nineties and looking back, it's not going
to be how much money you made or how many awards
you've won. It's really what did you stand for. Did you make
a positive difference for people?

ELIZABETH DOLE

Living one's "life purpose" is difficult for most people; it can feel like a puz-
zle with too many pieces. But discovering your life purpose is really not so
difficult—it essentially boils down to embracing the things that are important to you. The questions below will remind you of those passions and interests, leading naturally to discovering the greater purpose that will
motivate you forward. Find a quiet space where you won't be interrupted,
and take time to reflect on your answers.

- If you had more free time, how would you spend it?
- What experiences have moved you to tears of joy?
- What challenging global issues (e.g., poverty, religious intolerance,
  environmental decline, overpopulation) most trouble you?
- How do you want to be remembered? What legacy do you want
  to leave?
- If you were independently wealthy, how would you spend
  your time?
- If you could be famous for 10 minutes, what would you be
  acknowledged for?
- If you won the lottery tomorrow and received $10 million, how
  would you spend it and how would it change your current life?

WHAT IS YOUR LIFE WORK?

It's not work, if you love what you're doing.
Steve Sears

How many people do you know whose work is their passion or qualifies as their "life work"? Life work is different from a job or a profession. Life work is finding mental, emotional, and spiritual fulfillment in what you do. Our lives have greater meaning when our purpose and our jobs are consistent. When you bring your soul to work, what you are doing fulfills your inner yearnings beyond compensation or status. By doing what you love, you bring all of your energies into your tasks and your interactions with others.

The following questions will help you to determine whether your job/career has the qualities of life work:

- Do you love your job or career?
- Does it enable you to live a balanced life?
- Is your work helping to make the world a better place?
- What are you creating and committed to that is bigger than you?
- Do you have enough time to spend with the people you really care about?
- Does your life feel meaningful and are you guided by a sense of purpose?

If you've discovered that your work life is missing these qualities, then you need to make a job or career change, expand your perspective and view your contribution as a part of the bigger whole, and identify ways that you can create more balance in your life.

IMAGINE NEW POSSIBILITIES

We start out in our lives as little children, full of light and
the clearest vision.

BRENDA LELAND

Imagine that there are no limits to what you can create at this present moment. Imagine that anything is possible—quickly, easily, and now!

- Who would be in it?
- What would you be doing?
- Where would you be living?
- How would you feel?
- What would you look like?

FIVE STEPS TO MANIFESTING YOUR DESIRES

We are all visionaries, and what we see is our soul in things.
HENRY AMIEL

Step One: Determine what your goals are for the eight areas identified in the "Achieving a Life of Balance" wheel. If there are aspects of your life you would like to change, be very specific.

Step Two: Create a vision or mission statement that accurately describeswhat you're committed to contributing or learning in this lifetime.

Step Three: Create an action plan of how you're going to get there and the steps you need to take to turn this vision into reality.

Step Four: Break the vision or goal into small increments. If you want to own your home free and clear in 10 years, identify the progress you will have made in two years. Then break this down into yearly and monthly goals.

Step Five: Commit to keeping your goals alive and review them daily.

Now let's take those steps . . .

STEP ONE: ACHIEVING A LIFE OF BALANCE

Take time to think . . . It is the source of power.
Take time to play . . . It is the secret of perpetual youth.
Take time to laugh . . . It is the music of the soul.
Take time to pray . . . It is the greatest power on Earth.
WORDS WRITTEN ON THE WALL OF THE
MISSIONARIES OF CHARITY CHILDREN'S HOME,
CALCUTTA, INDIA

The following eight-spoked wheel represents eight key aspects of your life, and is a useful tool for assessing the balances and imbalances in your current situation.

ACHIEVING A LIFE OF BALANCE

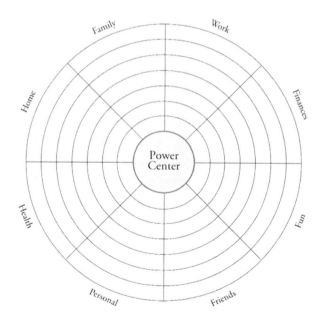

You can use this tool to help you identify where you're spending the majority of your time and energy, and which areas of your life you are neglecting. It will also help you design a plan that balances all of these areas, shifting the time you spend in one area to another as it reflects the changes you want to make in your life. Those eight areas are:

1. *Work*—your career, paid work, or volunteer and community work.
2. *Finances*—your wages from work, your investments, and your savings.
3. *Fun*—hobbies, sports, vacations, leisure-time movies, and time spent that's not focused on personal responsibilities.
4. *Friends*—your personal friends and your professional colleagues and co-workers.
5. *Personal*—time spent pursuing courses, books, formal or informal education, and spiritual and religious studies."
6. *Health*—your physical, mental, and emotional health.
7. *Home*—the house or apartment you live in as well as your city, town, or community.
8. *Family*—your significant other, children, relatives, and extended family.

In deciding what areas may need more time and attention, consider the following questions.

Work

- Is your job, career, or community work rewarding and fulfilling?
- Do you contribute your creative abilities at work?
- Are you acknowledged for your unique contributions?
- Are you making a difference?

Finances

- Do you have sufficient money to live the life you desire?
- If not, how much would you need to maintain your desired lifestyle?
- Do you have sufficient savings to handle an unexpected event?
- Do you have written financial goals?
- Do you have an action plan to achieve your goals?

Fun

- Do you have hobbies that you're passionate about?
- Do you have enough leisure time?
- Do you have enough time to engage in fun activities?
- Do you schedule down time to just do nothing?
- Is there a degree or certification you would like to pursue?

Friends

- How many close friends do you have?
- Do they support what you are committed to?
- Do they energize you and cause you to feel great about yourself? Or are they draining and depleting you of energy?
- Would you like to expand your circle of friends and professional colleagues?

Personal

- Do you take time to fix or replace personal items that need attention?
- Do you feel good about your personal appearance and presentation?
- What would you change that would help you to feel better about yourself?
- What area of personal growth would most benefit your life at this time?

- Do you take time to participate with your spiritual or religious community?

Health

- Do you make time to exercise?
- Do you set aside time to be outdoors and inspired by nature?
- Do you eat foods that support your health and energize you?
- Do you have specific goals for how you might commit to being healthier?
- Is your primary focus on preventing disease rather than on promoting greater levels of wellness?
- Do you have a regular practice that supports your overall well-being?

Home

- Does your home feel like a sanctuary from the busyness of life?
- Do you enjoy the city you live in, or would you like to move?
- Does the home or apartment you live in support your creative endeavors?
- Do you need to upgrade or change the environment you're living in?
- If you could create a new home, what would it look like and where would it be?

Family

- Do you have enough time to spend with your family?
- Or are you feeling overwhelmed and need a break?
- Do you have time to focus on the overall needs and health of your family?
- Do you have a plan that assures that the needs of all members are being met?
- Do you have family goals?

Time Allocation

Now let's take a look at your life: In the first graph, shade each of the eight areas based on the amount of focus and time you now allocate to it in your life. Shade each of the spokes to represent your degree of attention, so that the outer end of the spoke indicates a high degree of focus. The example will help you get started:

ACHIEVING A LIFE OF BALANCE

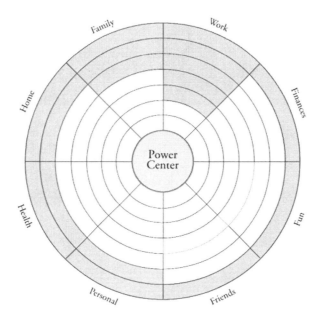

Do one or more aspects of your life consume most of your attention and energy?

Level of Satisfaction and Fulfillment

In the next graph, shade the eight areas based on the amount of satisfaction, fulfillment, or joy they give you. If you are not receiving any personal satisfaction from one of the areas, then it would not be shaded.

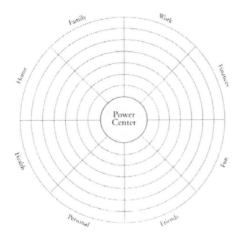

A Balanced Life

In this last graph, shade the eight areas based on what would be an ideal, less stressful balance (e.g., more fun, less work).

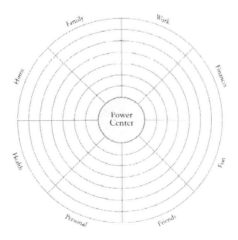

STEP TWO: POWER CENTER

Imagination is a very high sort of seeing.
RALPH WALDO EMERSON

The center of the wheel is marked "power center." This is the source of your personal strength and clarity; it is the energy that drives all of the eight areas of your life. It has been described as your higher self, your spiritual center, your higher consciousness, your expanded self, or even your "director." It helps you define your personal vision and mission. It's the same energy that enables people to tap into the wisdom of the universe and create great art, medical breakthroughs, and cutting-edge technologies. It is the energy that can change the world—*your* world—and everyone has this capacity.

However you refer to this source of personal power, it is the source that drives all of your actions on a daily basis. This personal power source helps you define your life purpose, life dreams, personal mission, or life vision. At some point in your life, you have tapped into this source to identify why you're here and what would give you the greatest amount of joy in life. But if you're like most of us, the busyness of life gets in the way and over time you forget that you possess this source of power, just as you forget your visions, life dreams, passions, and purpose.

For some, their source of power is their mission. A personal mission could be a spiritual calling, a self-imposed duty, or a passionate commitment to a cause. Nelson Mandela's mission was to end apartheid. Mother Teresa's mission was to show compassion to the dying. But personal missions do not have to affect large numbers of people or be grand. What's important is that they create meaning for your life. The value in having a mission statement is that it can guide your daily actions as well as your important decisions, and can enable you to decide more quickly whether an action is appropriate for you. Many individuals refer to this statement as their "vision." However you describe your primary motivator, writing your personal statement is an opportunity to decide what's really important to you. Mission and vision statements have no deadlines; they simply describe what you are committed to. To create a new life vision, the first step is to figure out what you really want—not what anyone else wants for you, but what would truly make *you* happy.

The following are some examples:

- "My mission is to inspire others through my artistic endeavors."
- "My vision is to create more beauty and harmony in the homes I decorate."
- "My mission is to create a work environment that enables my employees to realize their fullest potential."
- "My vision is to create more harmony in my family."

STEP THREE: SETTING GOALS

Your goal should be out of reach but not out of sight.
ANITA DEFRANTZ

To create change in your life, you need to focus on what you want, not on what you don't want. If you want to change your life but you keep focusing on what you don't want, you will just get more of the same. We create whatever we spend our time and energy thinking about. So to create a new job, buy a new house, or find the ideal partner, write down what you are committed to creating, but write it down in a way that describes how you will feel once you've attained your goal. Writing down your goals will support you in manifesting what you want more readily. Review them often; even 15 minutes a day will keep you committed to creating your new life.

Goals can help you to become more decisive and directed on a daily basis. They will help you focus your energies in a positive way to achieve the life you desire. Be specific about your goals and define them in as much detail as possible. For example, if your goal is to buy a new car, write down a specific model. Get a picture of the car you want and visualize yourself driving it. And while it's satisfying to have goals of being happy and successful, these goals can leave you feeling empty if they are not connected to contributing to others and making the world a safer or better place to live.

There is no question that it helps to have someone to guide your steps, especially at first. If hiring a coach is not in your budget, you definitely need a structure that will keep your goals, visions, and dreams on track. I believe everyone should revisit their life goals at least once a year. But individuals who are serious about being successful review and even make minor adjustments to their vision and goals on a weekly, monthly, and annual basis. To be effective, you need to be reminded of your goals daily. I find the best time is first thing in the morning. I sit down for 10 to 15 minutes and review what I'm committed to creating for the week, month, and year. Without this type of discipline, life happens and we get distracted. Then we wonder at the end of the year why life looks different from our intentions and goals. I also review my life purpose on a daily basis, to help me to stay focused and on target in my interactions with others.

For example, if your life purpose was focused on creating more harmony around you, whether among friends, neighbors, or your community, your perspective would be different as you traveled to work and it would definitely shift your daily work experience. If this was your purpose and you were committed to being mindful about it, the unpleasant events and circumstances you see on the road or even at your place of work would have little or no charge on your state of happiness. Individuals without a clear purpose are living at the effect of the rest of the world, or at least the part of it they come in contact with.

Review your goals daily. When you have decided on what you would like to accomplish for the next year, divide your yearly goals into monthly, quarterly, or seasonal goals. Here are several examples of ways to describe what you would like more of in your life:

- "I love the idea of living in a home near the water."
- "I enjoy my beautiful garden and the time I spend there."
- "I'm grateful for feeling strong and healthy and looking younger than my age. "
- "I'm blessed by having time to take care of my health."

Once you've identified what you really want and have written it down, determine the action steps you'll take to fulfill your vision. To keep your goals and commitments active, they should be active. You might also want to identify what you want to achieve by a certain date, such as when you turn 40, 50, 60, or 70. Once you have action items and a time frame, organize them into goals for the year. Then divide them again into three-month and one-month goals. (Worksheets at the end of this section will help you do this.) I find it's helpful to renew my goals on the last day of the month to prepare me for the next month. On Sundays, I set aside time to create my goals for the upcoming week.

The time spent on this activity will be well worth it, and the results will be valuable in every aspect of your life. Companies are in desperate need of visionaries at all levels of organizations, and the skills you develop will support your work environment.

STEPS FOUR AND FIVE:
ORGANIZING YOUR ACTION PLAN

The discipline of writing something down is the first step
to making it happen.

LEE IACOCCA

These worksheets will help you outline your goals and your action plan for achieving them. Please feel free to photocopy them as many times as you need, and write freely and honestly about what you want to do. Remember that your life mission can change with changing circumstances, and you may need to do this more than once before you reach your goal.

MY PLAN

My Life Purpose:

My Personal Vision:

My Life Work:

My Commitment is that my lifework will:

My Life Goals by the time I'm _____

1.

2.

3.

4.

or

What I Will Create by _____ (month, day, year)

MY GOALS AND FOCUS FOR _____ (YEAR)

Work

Finances

Fun

Friends

Personal

Health

Home

Family

MY GOALS FOR _____ (MONTH)

Work

Finances

Fun

Friends

Personal

Health

Home

Family

MY ACTION PLAN FOR MY GOALS
FOR _____ (YEAR OR MONTH)

Goal: _____ By: _____

Actions I Will Take:

    1.

    2.

    3.

    4.

Goal: _____ By: _____

Actions I Will Take:

    1.

    2.

    3.

    4.

Goal: _____ By: _____

Actions I Will Take:

    1.

    2.

    3.

    4.

Goal: _____ By: _____

Actions I Will Take:

    1.

    2.

    3.

    4.

Goal: _____ By: _____

Actions I Will Take:

    1.

    2.

    3.

    4.

Goal: _____ By: _____

Actions I Will Take:

    1.

    2.

    3.

    4.

AFFIRMATIONS

We always attract into our lives whatever we think about
most, believe in most strongly, expect on the deepest level,
and imagine most vividly.

SHAKTI GAWAIN

Your life up to this point in time is a result of how you have been thinking
about it. If you are not satisfied with your life but have been having difficulty creating new goals and a new lifestyle, it could be that you have been
programmed or conditioned by others to accept your status quo. If someone told you, you would never be successful, you may have come to believe
that they were right. In order to change that belief, you need to start re-pro-
gramming your subconscious mind. If you are not getting what you want in
life, you need to change the programming. It's important to plant affirma-
tive statements in your subconscious. Positive thoughts repeated over and
over in your mind will soon become a habitual way of thinking. A new
thought or message read several times a day for a week is virtually memo-
rized and recorded into your subconscious mind. Use these positive messages to help your goals become reality.

An affirmation is a thought of a desired condition. Since your environment
is a reflection of your thinking, you can change your reality when you change
your beliefs. The following are suggestions on how to use affirmations:

- State the affirmation as the desired condition, as if it is already
  happening—not "I want to get well and strong" but "I am healthy
  and getting stronger every day."
- Do not place a time limit on the affirmation. Allow it to happen in
  its own time.
- Write your affirmations on cards that you can carry in your wallet or
  purse, or tape onto your rear view or bathroom mirror.
- Read the affirmations every morning and each evening before going
  to sleep.

- Sing or chant your affirmation while driving in your car, and as often as possible.

Here are some examples of affirmations:

- I allow myself to be healthy, vibrant, and strong.
- I allow myself to enjoy the food and practices that keep my body healthy, energized, and vital.
- I allow myself to easily achieve and maintain my ideal body weight.
- I allow myself to easily and effectively communicate with my friends, family, and clients.
- I allow myself to lovingly support my friends, family, and clients in their growth and freedom.

Change is never easy, but if you commit yourself to it and enter into the process wholeheartedly, you will be amazed at what can be accomplished. Don't give up, and don't be impatient. This is *your life* you're working on!

ENERGY PRACTICES

Disclaimer

It is always best to begin a new practice under the guidance of a trained professional. It is also important to listen to your body before doing any exercises. Millions of dollars would be saved every day if we had more training in listening to our bodies. If you are in pain, have injuries or have recently been in an accident or been hospitalized you should consult your health practitioner prior to doing any of the yoga exercises.

BREATHING

Individuals who have participated in the energy practices of yoga, Chi Gung or energy-focused meditation often quickly learn the importance of breathing correctly. Most of us have not been taught to breathe with our diaphragms so we don't understand its importance. While my brothers and I were growing up, my grandfather, an expert swimmer, constantly pointed out that we were not breathing properly and instructed us in diaphragmatic breathing.

One of the leading experts on breathwork who teaches how breathing promotes physical, mental and spiritual well-being is Gay Hendricks, M.D. In his book *Conscious Breathing,* he describes a problem he believes to be universal, which is that people tense their bellies as they breathe so that the diaphragm does not move freely. He states, "According to one medical researcher, poor breathing plays a role in more than 75 percent of the ills people bring to their doctors. In most cases, poor diaphragmatic breathing is the culprit."

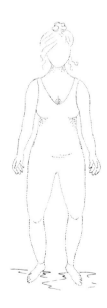

The following are two of the breathing practices from Michael Sky's book, *The Power of Emotion*. The first is the Belly Breath, which is practiced in most forms of meditation, yoga and Chi Gung.

The Belly Breath

Now, even as you read, bring attention to the movement of your breath. Breathe in deeply through your nose, filling your torso, and breathe out through the mouth in a long, soft, hushing sound, sssshhhh . . . Let the air go all the way out, without tensing, until you can no longer make the sound, and then breathe in deeply through your nose, filling your torso, and breathe out through the mouth in a long, soft, hushing sssshhhh . . . Now, as you continue this breathing, pay attention to the movements of your lower belly. As you breathe in, allow your belly to expand, becoming full and round with vital energy. As you breathe out, your belly empties and flattens, sssshhhh . . . Every breath in, your belly expands; every breath out, your belly empties, sssshhhh . . . Continue this breathing, these deep, gentle breaths, your belly rhythmically expanding and emptying, even as you read. . . .

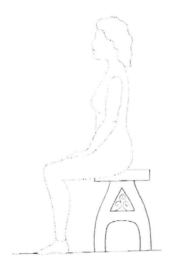

The following breathing practice involves visualization and is particularly helpful if you are feeling anxious or agitated. Note your breath will be chest focused but be sure to bring breath to your belly as well.

The Radiant Heart Breath

Now even as you read, bring attention to the movement of your breath. Breathe in deeply through your nose, filling your torso, and breathe out through the mouth in a long, soft, gentle sssshhhh. . . .

Again, breathe in deeply through your nose, filling your torso, and breathe out through the mouth in a long, soft, gentle sssshhhh. . . .

Now, continuing with this breathing, feel or sense or imagine that as you inhale, energy flows into and fills your heart, the center of your chest, and as you exhale the energy radiates out from the heart in all directions. . . .

Inhaling, your heart fills with energy, exhaling, the energy radiates out from the heart, as light from a star. . . .

Continue with several long, slow, gentle heart breaths, and as you breathe, think about or remember some person whom you deeply love. . . .

Let this breathing into and from the heart become a gentle movement of love energy.

Inhaling, your heart fills with love energy.

Exhaling, love energy radiates out from the heart, as light from a star. . . .

Continue with several long, slow, gentle heart breaths, filling with love energy, radiating love energy, even as you read. . . .

Michael speaks of emotional energy as a river circulating through all parts of our body:

> Your whole emotional experience arises from the one flowing river of energy. Suppress any part of the river and all of your emotions— inward flowing and outward expanding—must suffer. Suppress any feelings of sadness and your capacity for love diminishes. Suppress any feelings of anger and your capacity for love diminishes. Suppress any emotion—positive or negative, easy or difficult—and your whole emotional experience, including and especially your capacity for love, diminishes.

SCANNING YOUR BODY

We can use our breath to increase our energy as well as create a greater degree of calm and relaxation. Breathing can be used to release the tension we
naturally accumulate during the day.

After you have practiced the breathing exercises described previously,
remain in your sitting or lying posture with your eyes closed. Scan your
body for areas of tension or pressure. Using slow, deep breathing, focus
your attention on these areas of tension and visualize the tension releasing
as you exhale your breath, and breathe new energy into these areas of your
body as you inhale.

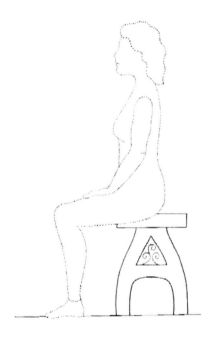

YOGIC THREE-PART BELLY BREATH

There are many ways to use the breath in yoga and the one I am presenting also has benefits in the complete reverse. I have presented the belly breath because in our culture, we tend to hold our bellies taut, creating tension in the diaphragm and the organs of the abdomen. It is believed that many emotions reside here, so giving them space through belly breathing allows release.

While in your lying posture with your eyes closed, place your hands on your belly. As you inhale, feel your belly rise into your hands. As you exhale, feel your belly release back toward the floor. Do this until you're comfortable. Now leave one hand on your belly and place the other on your ribs. As you inhale, feel first your belly expand, then your ribs. As you exhale, release first from the ribs, then the belly. Do this until it is comfortable. The final step is to place the hand now on your belly onto your chest. Inhale first into your belly, then ribs, then your chest, feeling all of these areas expand. On the exhale, release first from the chest, then ribs, then the belly. Do this breathing practice ten times.

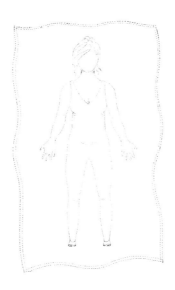

BASIC BUDDHIST MEDITATION

To begin meditation, select a quiet time and place. Be seated on a cushion that gives three or four inches of firm support under your sit bones, or on a chair, taking an erect yet balanced and relaxed posture. Let yourself sit upright with the quiet dignity of a king or queen. Close your eyes gently and begin by bringing a full, present attention to whatever you feel and hear within you and around you. Let your mind be spacious and your heart be kind and soft.

Jack Kornfield was trained as a Buddhist monk in Thailand and Burma, and has taught around the world since 1974. He is the author of several books, including *Buddha's Little Instruction Book*, from which the following meditation practice has been taken:

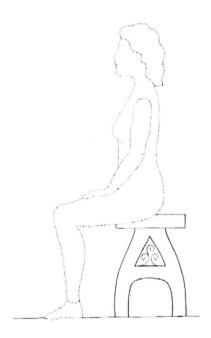

Let Your Mind Settle
Like a Clear Forest Pool

As you sit, feel the sensations of your body. Then notice what sounds and feelings, thoughts and expectations are present. Allow them all to come and go, to rise and fall like the waves of the ocean. Be aware of the waves, and rest seated in the midst of them. Allow yourself to become more and more still.

In the center of all these waves, feel your breathing, your life-breath. Let your attention feel the in-and-out breathing wherever you notice it, as coolness or tingling in the nose or throat, as a rising and falling of your chest or abdomen. Relax and softly rest your attention on each breath, feeling the movement in a steady, easy way. Let the breath breathe itself in any rhythm, long or short, soft or deep. As you feel each breath, concentrate and settle into its movement. Let all other sounds and sensations, thoughts and feelings continue to come and go like waves in the background.

ENERGY MEDITATION AND THE CHAKRAS

Chakra or energy meditation enables you to balance and energize your body's chakras. The seven spinning energy centers regulate your physical, mental, emotional and spiritual well-being. This type of meditation is appropriate when you need to recharge and renew your energy. Chakras are our focal point for our feelings and intuition. Each chakra has its own characteristics and is connected to different organs in the body. By focusing on the corresponding color of each of the seven chakras through a meditative visualization, you can tune and realign your whole body.

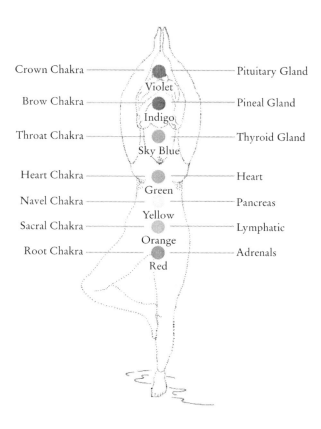

Crown Chakra — Violet — Pituitary Gland

Brow Chakra — Indigo — Pineal Gland

Throat Chakra — Sky Blue — Thyroid Gland

Heart Chakra — Green — Heart

Navel Chakra — Yellow — Pancreas

Sacral Chakra — Orange — Lymphatic

Root Chakra — Red — Adrenals

Chakra		Location	Color	Glands/Organs
1st	Root *or* Base	Base of the spine	Red	Adrenals/ Kidneys, Colon
2nd	Sacral Plexus *or* Navel	Lower abdomen	Orange	Lymphatic/ Bladder, Spleen, Genitals
3rd	Solar Plexus	Between the navel and chest	Yellow	Pancreas/ Stomach, Gallbladder, Liver
4th	Heart	Center of the chest	Green	Heart/ Lungs, Thymus
5th	Throat	Throat area	Sky Blue	Thyroid/ Throat, Hypothalamus
6th	Brow (Third Eye)	Between the eyebrows	Indigo (Dark Blue)	Pineal/ Eyes, Ears, Nose
7th	Crown	Top of the head	Violet	Pituitary/ Central Nervous System

CHAKRA MEDITATION

By meditating on each chakra, you can balance your whole body. A variety of techniques have been created that focus on balancing energy through the chakras.

The following meditation includes the basic principles of these practices.

Sit in a relaxed position as you would for any meditation with your eyes closed. Take some deep breaths and notice how your breath enters your nose, then fills your lungs and then is released.

Visualize a large brilliant sphere of light above your head. First picture a bright red sphere of light and draw the energy of this light to the root chakra at the base of your spine. The color of this chakra is red and it governs your physical health and vitality.

Take a moment to notice this area of your body. Imagine a brilliant red swirling vortex of energy surrounding this area of your spine. Visualize this whirling red vortex releasing thoughts, feelings and emotions that no longer serve you. Notice the tingling sensation as this chakra becomes clear and vibrant.

Repeat this process for each chakra.

Scan your body to see if you are perfectly balanced. If you feel a blockage in a specific area of your body, visualize a sphere of brilliant white or golden light that is the essence of love surrounding the area of your body that still feels tense. Imagine that this golden white light of love is healing and releasing the tension in this area of your body.

You should now feel refreshed, calm and renewed. Your energy is in balance and you are full of vitality. Visualize yourself as perfectly balanced and filled with inner strength. For those who are particularly sensitive to toxic environments:

Imagine that you are completely surrounded and filled with a golden white light. Imagine this light extending two feet out and around your body. Visualize a silver shield that is providing you with strength and protection so that only positive energy will come to you.

In the middle of a busy day, and in particular when dealing with a challenging situation, notice which part of your body feels tense in reaction to an upsetting event. Focus your attention on the color and chakra closely aligned with that part of the body. Practice the chakra meditation for just that one area of your body for a quick release and grounding. This should support you in moving forward.

TAOIST WAYS TO TRANSFORM
STRESS INTO VITALITY:
THE MICROCOSMIC ORBIT

Illness is caused by a blockage of energy. Too much or too little energy in one part of the body results in disease of that part and stresses the entire body. The Healing Tao teaches us how to correct this imbalance by awakening the chi, or vital energy, and circulating it to the needed areas.

MANTAK CHIA

A powerful body of work is that of Mantak Chia, a Taoist master. Born in Thailand, Master Chia developed his personal system, the Healing Tao, in his native land in the early 1970s, and introduced it to the West in 1979 when he opened the Healing Tao Center in New York. He is the author of numerous books and has gone on to establish Taoist centers throughout the United States and Europe.

Master Chia describes Taoism as "the mother of acupuncture and the inspiration for modern body-oriented therapies, such as acupressure, Rolfing, and Feldenkrais." His work incorporates both meditative practices and physical disciplines such as Chi Kung (a spelling variation of Chi Gung).

The Taoists have been studying the subtle energy points in the body for thousands of years. It is believed that the Microcosmic Orbit loop will carry energy to all of the organs in the body, clear the channel of physical or mental blockages, and spread vitality to other parts of the body.

The process is one of pumping life force energy down the front meridian points of the body and back up the spine, through what Master Chia refers to as the channel. The channel starts at the crown of the head and continues down through the mid-eyebrow, the throat area, the heart, the solar plexus, the navel, and the sexual organs, then back to the base of the sacrum, up to the kidney meridian, and through the back of the heart area to the back of the skull, ending at the crown of the head. The tongue acts like a switch that connects the front channel to the back channel. When the tongue is touching the roof of the mouth, behind the back teeth, the energy will flow in a circle up the spine and down the front meridians.

The practice is best done after meditating or some basic breathing such as the Belly Breath. The key is to simply relax and bring the awareness to the part of the loop being focused on. In this way, we can easily experience the energy flowing to the different parts of the body. The practice not only promotes the vital flow of energy but can also contribute to slowing the aging process and healing stress-related illnesses.

The following diagram is provided with Master Chia's permission. A more extensive description of this practice can be found in his book, *Taoist Ways to Transform Stress Into Vitality: The Inner Smile—Six Healing Sounds.*

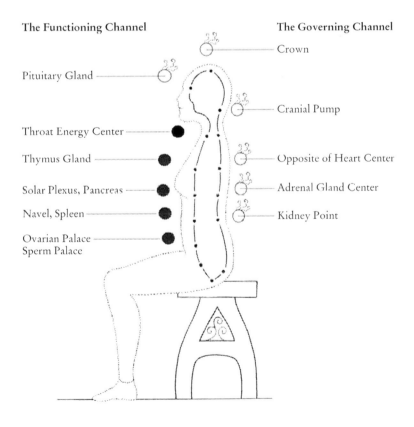

The Functioning Channel — The Governing Channel

Crown

Pituitary Gland

Cranial Pump

Throat Energy Center

Thymus Gland — Opposite of Heart Center

Solar Plexus, Pancreas — Adrenal Gland Center

Navel, Spleen — Kidney Point

Ovarian Palace
Sperm Palace

TONING AND THE POWER OF HARMONICS

When a part of our body or an organ located in a specific area of our body is healthy, it will create a resonant frequency that harmonizes with the rest of the body. But when disease is present, a different sound pattern will be created, which will not vibrate in harmony with the rest of the body.

When we create sound through the use of toning, and direct this sound to a specific area of the body that is stressed or diseased, we are reintroducing a new and more aligned harmonic pattern. "Toning" is the use of the voice as an instrument for healing. It is a term first used by Laurel Elizabeth Keyes in her book, *Toning*, which has now become something of a classic in this field of sound healing. According to Keyes, "Toning is an ancient method of healing . . . the idea is to restore people to their harmonic patterns." Jonathan Goldman, director of The Sound Healers Association Inc., lectures, teaches and produces meditational and healing music that he describes as "sonic yoga" for meditation and deep relaxation.

While chanting uses words that are part of religious texts that have a specific meaning, toning is non-verbal sound, which primarily utilizes vowels. The practice of toning may be done sitting or standing and may be easier to start with by sitting in a chair or sitting cross-legged on the floor. Whether sitting or standing, it's important that the spine is straight and that you are relaxed.

Sit in a relaxed position as you would for any meditation with your eyes closed. Take some deep breaths and notice how your breath enters your nose, then fills your lungs and then is released.

To create a tone or sound, inhale through your nose, and when you release your breath through your mouth, make a sustained sound. You might start by using the sound ahhhh.

When you are making a sound, make sure the muscles in your face, neck and jaw are relaxed. Experiment with different vowels, notes and intensities.

Find a tone and a note that you like and repeat the sound again and again.

While there are numerous interpretations of specific vowel sounds associated with different parts of the body, our bodies naturally know which sounds, notes and vowels will bring us back into proper alignment.

The following diagram illustrates Jonathan Goldman's system of using vowel sounds to resonate chakras.

He also suggests that you visualize a color while focusing on the sound.

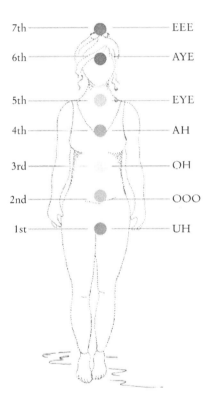

7th	EEE
6th	AYE
5th	EYE
4th	AH
3rd	OH
2nd	OOO
1st	UH

From Jonathan Goldman, *Healing Sounds: The Power of Harmonics*

MANTRA

The short version of the Tibetan Buddhist mantra is OM. Longer versions of mantras are:

Zen Buddhist

GATE, GATE, PARAGATE, PARASAMGATE, BODHI SVAHA
This Sanskrit mantra is the last line of the *Heart of Wisdom* sutra, and is translated as, "Gone, gone, gone beyond, gone so far to the other shore, free is the mind."

Tibetan Buddhist

The following is a Tibetan Buddhist prayer for enlightenment. "Mani" means jewel and refers to wisdom. "Padma" is the Sanskrit word for lotus. "Hum" represents the wisdom mind of The Buddha and brings divinity and spirituality into reality on Earth.

OM MANI PADMA HUM

Popular Modern Mantras

We are one with the infinite sun
Forever and ever and ever

This little light of mine I'm going to make it shine
This little light of mine I'm going to make it shine
This little light of mine I'm going to make it shine
Let it shine, let it shine, let it shine

RESTORATIVE POSE—WALL SERIES

This series is good for someone who is tired from a hectic day and especially for those who are on their feet all day. They can be done right before going to bed or when you need a deep rest before going out in the evening. The wall series are poses done by placing your legs up against a wall. They are more comfortable if done on a carpeted floor or on a padded yoga mat. Additional stretching and release can be created by placing a blanket at the base of the spine.

Take five deep full breaths in the beginning of each posture, then let the breath go for several minutes before transitioning to the next posture. If you plan to go to sleep right after this practice, lengthen the exhale, only to the extent it is comfortable. If you want to increase your energy, lengthen the inhale, only to the extent it is comfortable.

Legs straight

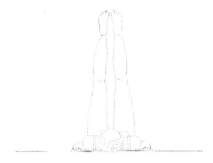

Legs separated into a V

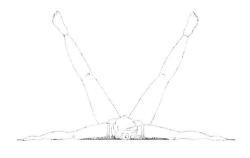

Feet together

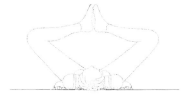

One leg crossed over the other

Return to legs straight

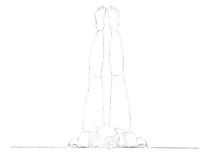

To end this series, hug your knees, and roll to one side to get up.

FLOOR AND STANDING SERIES

The floor series is very good for tense backs and is more comfortable if practiced on a rug, carpet or yoga mat. To start, lie on your back away from any walls or furniture.

1. Bring your knees to your chest and cup your hands over your knees. Draw your knees gently into your chest while you exhale, and then release them away from your chest, on the inhale. Do this five times.

2. While cupping your hands over your knees, create circles with your knees doing several slow clockwise movements, and then the same number of movements in a counter clockwise direction. As your knees are moving away from you, inhale, as they are moving towards you, exhale. Do this three times in each direction.

3. With your arms resting at your side, bring your knees to your chest
   on the exhale. On the inhale, raise your arms over your head while
   extending both of your legs towards the ceiling, but keeping your
   legs slightly bent. Do this five times.

4. With your knees bent, place your feet slightly wider than the width
   of your body. First gently move both knees to the left, emphasizing
   moving the right knee forward and toward the floor. Exhale as you
   are moving your knee towards the floor. Then inhale as you change
   sides. Do this five times on each side.

5. Hug both knees to your chest for three breaths.

6. This stretch is often referred to as "cat cow." This practice is beneficial for those with tight backs. First, inhale lifting your head up and opening your chest while slightly releasing your abdomen towards the ground like an old cow. Second, slowly exhale while your head moves back down and your spine reaches up to the sky, rounding your back like an upset cat. Release your head and neck completely on the exhale. Do this five times.

7. The last of the floor stretches is the extended child. This is very good for stretching the shoulders. Release the forhead to the ground and release the neck. Take three breaths in this position.

8. Returning to a standing position, shrug your shoulders up towards your ears, then release completely.

    Do this five times.

9. Breath of Joy. Clasp your hands together at your chest—this position is often referred to as Namasté. In many Asian cultures it is a form of greeting, which means, "The light in me honors the light in you."

Clasp your fingers on the inhale.

Press your palms forward,
fingers interlaced on the exhale.

Extend your palms over your head
on the inhale with your fingers interlaced
and your palms facing the ceiling.

Release your arms letting
them float down to your
sides on the exhale.

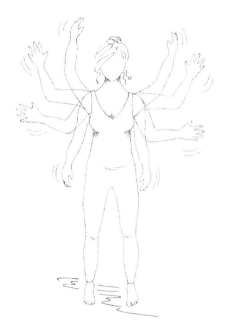

Clasp your hands behind your back, opening your chest on the inhale.

Exhale while returning back to Namasté.

10. Lie on the floor in savasana, the resting pose. This is referred to as the corpse pose, as in this state of relaxation, the body should be as still as a corpse and the mind is at peace. If lying in this position for an extended period of time, covering yourself with a blanket would be helpful in keeping you warm. The arms are out slightly away from the trunk of the body with the palms up. Close your eyes and return to normal and restful breathing. Let the body sink into the ground. Rest quietly for five or ten minutes.

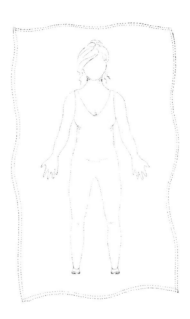

YOGA STRETCHES

Salute to the Moon — Ardha Chandrasana

The salute to the moon, Ardha Chandrasana, is a series of twenty-one stretching positions, many of which are commonly found in warm-up exercises.

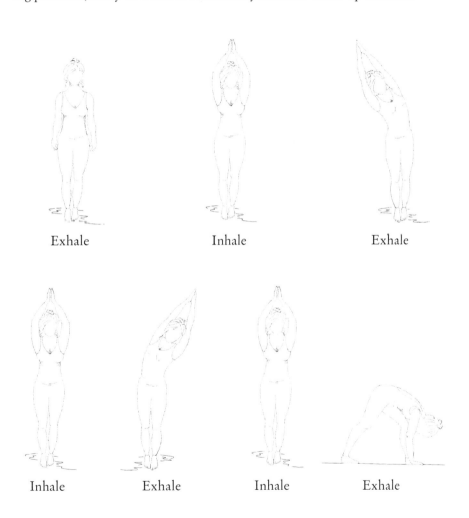

Exhale   Inhale   Exhale

Inhale   Exhale   Inhale   Exhale

Inhale   Exhale   Inhale

Exhale   Inhale   Exhale

Inhale   Exhale

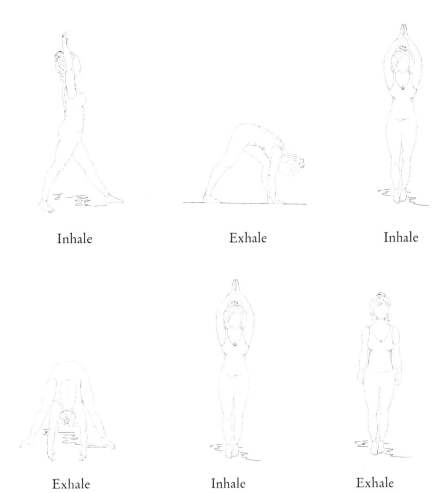

Inhale   Exhale   Inhale

Exhale   Inhale   Exhale

WORDS OF WISDOM
AND INSPIRATION

The following section is a collection of words of wisdom. The passages are meant for reflection and inspiration. The reading of scriptures and prayers of the world's spiritual and religious beliefs can be used to promote a more positive outlook on life. As we are surrounded with negative images daily, the reading of these passages can remind us of our own higher potential. They would be most beneficial when read right before retiring for the evening.

PRAYER OF SAINT FRANCIS

FRANCIS BERNADONE (ST. FRANCIS OF ASSISI)
Born in Assisi, Italy, in 1180

Lord, make me an instrument of thy peace.
Where there is hatred, let me sow love;
Where there is injury, pardon;
Where there is doubt, faith;
Where there is despair, hope;
Where there is darkness, light;
And where there is sadness, joy.

O Divine Master, grant that I may not
so much seek to be consoled as to console,
To be understood as to understand,
To be loved as to love;
For it is in giving that we receive;
It is in pardoning that we are pardoned;
And it is in dying to self that we are born to eternal life.

DISCOURSE ON GOOD WILL

The Buddha
from *The Sutta Nipata*

May all beings be filled with joy and peace.
May all beings everywhere,
The strong and the weak,
The great and the small,
The mean and the powerful,
The short and the long,
The subtle and the gross:

May all beings everywhere,
Seen and unseen,
Dwelling far off or nearby,
Being or waiting to become:
May all be filled with lasting joy.

Let no one deceive another,
Let no one anywhere despise another,
Let no one out of anger or resentment
Wish suffering on anyone at all.

Just as a mother with her own life
Protects her child, her only child, from harm,
So within yourself let grow
A boundless love for all creatures.

Let your love flow outward through the universe,
To its height, its depth, its broad extent,
A limitless love, without hatred or enmity.

Then, as you stand or walk,
Sit or lie down,
As long as you are awake,
Strive for this with a one-pointed mind;
Your life will bring heaven to earth.

THE SHEMA

from THE TORAH

Hear O Israel,
    the Lord our God, the Lord is one.
    blessed is his name,
    whose glorious kingdom is forever.

And you shall love the Lord with all your heart, and with all your
soul, and with all your might.

And these words, which I command you this day, shall be upon
your heart;

And you shall teach them always to your children, and shall talk of them
when you sit in your house, when you walk by the way,
when you lie down, and when you arise.

And you shall bind them as a sign on your hand, and they will be
seen as a badge between your eyes.

And you shall write them on the doorposts of your house, and
upon your gates.

These segments of the Torah have been recited together since Biblical times
as the central affirmation of the Jewish faith. Tradition prescribes that the Shema
be spoken "with entire collection and concentration of heart and mind." This
translation is by Ellen Lehmann Beeler.

FINDING UNITY

LAO TZU

Those who know do not speak;
Those who speak do not know.
Stop up the openings,
Close down the doors,
Rub off the sharp edges.
Unravel all confusion,
Harmonize the light,
Give up contention:
This is called finding the unity of life.

When love and hatred cannot affect you,
Profit and loss cannot touch you,
Praise and blame cannot ruffle you,
You are honored by all the world.

Chapter 56 of the *Tao Te Ching*, a collection of verses about Tao—"The Way," the indivisible unity of life ascribed to the Chinese mystic Lao Tzu, who lived in the sixth century B.C. This translation is by Stephen Ruppenthal.

ANO ANO ("THE SEED")

KRISTIN ZAMBUCKA

We are all on a spiral path.
No growth takes place in a straight line.
There will be setbacks along the way . . .
There will be shadows, but they will be balanced by patches
    of light and fountains of joy as we grow and progress.
Awareness of the pattern is all you need to sustain you along the way . . .

Spirit alone is immortal.
Man is made up of ideas . . . and ideas will guide his life.
The physical body is lent to us so that spirit may come into
    contact with matter.
Neither worship that body nor neglect it . . .
But respect the instrument you have been given to pursue
    this earthly life.

From an inspirational work written and illustrated by Kristin Zambucka, dedicated to the Hawaiians' spiritual journey. In *Ano Ano*, an imaginary group of seekers asks questions and receives answers that give them hope.

TIBETAN PRAYER:
FROM THE TIBETAN YUNGDRUNG BÖN TRADITION

Lama Khemsar Rinpoche

In the Lama, Enlightened Ones, Teachings, and Spiritual Warriors,
  I seek refuge until the attainment of enlightenment.
To liberate all the sentient beings, who are as one's Mother, from the
  ocean of suffering, I generate in myself the Sublime Mind of
enlightenment.

May all the sentient beings that are encompassed by the sky be
  enriched with happiness and the cause of happiness.

May all sentient beings be parted from suffering and the cause
  of suffering.

May all sentient beings be never parted from the happiness of that
  nonsuffering state.

May the mind of all sentient beings abide in the state of equipoise
  parted from both suffering and nonsuffering.

From Timothy Freke, *Shamanic Wisdomkeepers: Shamanism in the Modern World*

CELTIC PRAYER

Andy Baggott

I call upon the four winds,
Earth to ground me,
Air to teach me,
Fire to empower me,
Water to uplift me.

I honor Grandmother Earth who bore me,
Grandfather Sky who watches over me,
And the Creator whose spark
Is within me and all things.

From Timothy Freke, *Shamanic Wisdomkeepers: Shamanism in the Modern World*

ON WORK

KAHLIL GIBRAN
From his masterpiece, *The Prophet*

Then a ploughman said, Speak to us of Work.

And he answered, saying:

You work that you may keep pace with the earth and the soul of
the earth.

For to be idle is to become a stranger unto the seasons, and to step
out of life's procession, that marches in majesty and proud
submission towards the infinite.

When you work you are a flute through whose heart the whispering
of the hours turns to music.

Which of you would be a reed, dumb and silent, when all else sings
together in unison?

Always you have been told that work is a curse and labour a misfortune.

But I say to you that when you work you fulfill a part of earth's furthest
dream, assigned to you when that dream was born,

And in keeping yourself with labour you are in truth loving life,

And to love life through labour is to be intimate with life's inmost secret.

But if you in your pain call birth an affliction and the support of the flesh
a curse written upon your brow, then I answer that naught but the sweat
of your brow shall wash away that which is written.

You have been told also that life is darkness, and in your weariness
you echo what was said by the weary.

And I say that life is indeed darkness save when there is urge.

And all urge is blind save when there is knowledge,

And all knowledge is vain save when there is work,
And all work is empty save when there is love;
And when you work with love you bind yourself to yourself, and to
one another, and to God.

And what is it to work with love?
It is to weave the cloth with threads drawn from your heart, even
as if your beloved were to wear that cloth.
It is to build a house with affection, even as if your beloved were to
dwell in that house.
It is to sow seeds with tenderness and reap the harvest with joy, even
as if your beloved were to eat the fruit.
It is to charge all things you fashion with a breath of your own spirit,
And to know that all the blessed dead are standing about you and watching.

Often have I heard you say, as if speaking in sleep, "He who works in
marble, and finds the shape of his own soul in the stone, is nobler
than he who ploughs the soil.
And he who seizes the rainbow to lay it on a cloth in the likeness of man,
is more than he who makes the sandals for our feet."

But I say, not in sleep but in the over-wakefulness of noontide, that the
wind speaks not more sweetly to the giant oaks than to the least
of all the blades of grass.

And he alone is great who turns the voice of the wind into a song made
sweeter by his own loving.

Work is love made visible.

And if you cannot work with love but only with distaste, it is better that
you should leave your work and sit at the gate of the temple and
take alms of those who work with joy.
For if you bake bread with indifference, you bake a bitter bread that
feeds but half man's hunger.

And if you grudge the crushing of the grapes, your grudge distils a
poison in the wine.
And if you sing though as angels, and love not the singing, you
muffle man's ears to the voices of the day and the voices of the night.

THE REAL WORK

Rumi
From *The Illuminated Rumi:*
Translations & Commentary by Coleman Barks

There is one thing in this world that you must never forget to do. If you forget everything else and not this, there's nothing to worry about; but if you remember everything else and forget this, then you will have done nothing in your life.

It's as if a king has sent you to some country to do a task, and you perform a hundred other services, but not the one he sent you to do. So human beings come to this world to do particular work. That work is the purpose, and each is specific to the person. If you don't do it, it's as though a priceless Indian sword were used to slice rotten meat. It's a golden bowl being used to cook turnips, when one filing from the bowl could buy a hundred suitable pots. It's a knife of the finest tempering nailed into a wall to hang things on.

You say, "But look, I'm using the dagger. It's not lying idle."

Do you hear how ludicrous that sounds? For a penny, an iron nail could be bought to serve the purpose. You say, "But I spend my energies on lofty enterprises. I study jurisprudence and philosophy and logic and astronomy and medicine and all the rest." But consider why you do those things. They are all branches of yourself.

Remember the deep root of your being, the presence of your lord. Give your life to the one who already owns your breath and your moments. If you don't you will be exactly like the man who takes a precious dagger and hammers it into his kitchen wall for a peg to hold his dipper gourd. You'll be wasting valuable keenness and foolishly ignoring your dignity and your purpose.

THE BHAGAVAD GITA—THE ILLUMINED MAN

From *God Makes the Rivers to Flow:*
Sacred Literature of the World,
selected by Eknath Easwaran

Arjuna:
    Tell me of the one who lives in wisdom,
    Ever aware of the Self, O Krishna;
    How does he talk, how sit, how move about?

Sri Krishna:
    He lives in wisdom
    Who sees himself in all and all in him,
    Whose love for the Lord of Love has consumed
    Every selfish desire and sense craving
    Tormenting the heart. Not agitated
    By grief nor hankering after pleasure,
    He lives free from lust and fear and anger.
    Fettered no more by selfish attachments,
    He is not elated by good fortune
    Nor depressed by bad. Such is the seer.

    Even as a tortoise draws in its limbs
    The sage can draw in his senses at will.
    An aspirant abstains from sense-pleasures,
    But he still craves for them. These cravings all
    Disappear when he sees the Lord of Love.

    For even of one who treads the path
    The stormy senses can seep off the mind.
    But he lives in wisdom who subdues them,
    And keeps his mind ever absorbed in me.

He is forever free who has broken out
Of the ego-cage of I and mine
To be united with the Lord of Love.
This is the supreme state. Attain thou this
And pass from death to immortality.

THE SIGNS AND SYMPTOMS OF INNER PEACE

Anonymous
From *Spirit of Health Newsletter* (date unknown)

A tendency to think and act spontaneously, rather than responding to fears based on past experience

An unmistakable ability to enjoy each moment

A loss of interest in judging other people

A loss of interest in interpreting the actions of others

A loss of ability to worry

Frequent, overwhelming episodes of appreciation

Contented feelings of connectedness with others and frequent attacks of smiling

An increasing susceptibility to the love extended by others as an uncontrollable urge to extend it

ACKNOWLEDGMENTS

Acknowledgments

I'm grateful for the many people who have supported my writing: Mathew Gilbert, for his general publishing advice and developmental editing expertise; Patty Monoco, for her impeccable copy editing; Layla Smith Bockhorst, for her on-going editorial input; Sonia Nordenson, for her initial editorial input that enabled the book to take shape; Linda Roggensack, for preliminary copy editing and input on content; Laura Egan, for her delightful graphic designs; Marilyn McGuire, for her invaluable input; Dee Hein, for her critique of the yoga graphics and discussions; and Michael Sky, for his writing coaching. My appreciation for the life stories that were contributed by Michelle Gasper, Mathew Gilbert, and Marilyn McGuire, and others who gave permission to share their stories anonymously.

I also want to thank the individuals who took time out of their busy schedules to read initial drafts and provide me with valuable insights that helped shape the book: Moriah Armstrong, Jill Blankenship, Artha Kass, Marci Cohen, John Clancy, Patricia Flores, Lynette Friberg, Gretchen Grani, Linda Roggensack, Elizabeth Roulac, Janis Mason Steeves, and Leota Shaner.

I would like to extend special thanks and gratitude to the many teachers and energy healers that I have had the privilege to study and work with, and to benefit from their talents. In particular I would like to acknowledge: Pam Adler, Carol Adrienne, Angeles Arrien, Sahn Ashena, Sherry Brier, Richard Brier, Carol Proudfoot-Edgar, Ann Farbman, Thict Nhat Hanh, Michael Harner, Sandra Harner, Dee Hein, Sandra Ingerman, Mary Ingersoll, Robert Jangaard, Joan Jerman, Helen Joseph, Michael Joseph, JoAnne Kellert, Tom Kenyon, Donna

Laslo, Daniel Lewis, Gay Luce, Theresa Lumiere, Susan Osborn, David Patten, Larry Peters, Jill Purce, and Sobunfu Some.

I want to acknowledge members of my family for their unique gifts and inspiration, and for providing me valuable life lessons: my brother, Stephen Roulac, for his unparalleled discipline and mastery; my brother, James Roulac, for his commitment to teaching and demonstrating our connection to nature; my sister, Joan Roulac, for her enthusiastic outlook and commitment to teaching the benefits of T'ai Chi Chuh; my brother, John Roulac, for his courage and commitment to promoting greater harmony on this planet through his healthy products; my son, Kevin Grani, for his ability to demonstrate responsible actions in all areas of his life; my daughter, Gretchen Grani, for her commitment to creating more beauty and order in a chaotic world; and my grandsons, Jason and Cole Seavey, for inspiring me to make a difference. Finally, I am indebted to my clients and workshop participants, from whom I am forever learning valuable life lessons.

BIBLIOGRAPHY

BIBLIOGRAPHY

Allen, James, *As a Man Thinketh*. Los Angeles: DeVorss & Co. (1910) 1979.

Arrien, Angeles, Ph.D., *The Four-Fold Way: Walking the Paths of the Warrior, Teacher, Healer and Visionary*. New York: Harper Collins Publishers, 1993.

_____, *Focus* magazine article, 1997.

Baggott, Andy [with, Dr. Andrew Tressider, consultant], *The Encyclopedia of Energy Healing: A Complete Guide to Using the Major Forms of Healing for the Body, Mind and Spirit*. New York: Sterling Publishing Company, Inc., 1999.

Barks, Coleman, *The Illuminated Rumi: Translations and Commentary*. New York: Broadway Books, a division of Bantam Doubleday Dell, 1997.

Borysenko, Joan, Ph.D., *Healers on Healing*. New York: Jeremy P. Tarcher/Putnam, 1989.

Braden, Gregg, *Walking Between the Worlds: the Science of Compassion*. Bellevue, Washington: Radio Bookstore Press, 1997.

_____, *The Isaiah Effect: Decoding The Lost Science of Prayer and Prophecy*. New York: Three Rivers Press, 2000.

Buckingham, Marcus and Donald O. Clifton, *Now, Discover Your Strengths: The revolutionary program that shows you how to develop your unique talents and strengths—and those of the people you manage. Based on the Gallup study of over two million people*. New York: The Free Press, a Division of Simon & Schuster Inc., 2001.

Cameron, Julia, *The Sound of Paper: Starting from Scratch*. New York: Jeremy P. Tarcher Penguin, 2004.

Campbell, Don, *The Mozart Effect: Tapping the Power of Music to Heal the Body, Strengthen the Mind and Unlock the Creative Spirit.* New York: Avon Books, Inc., 1997.

Carlson, Richard, Ph.D., Shield, Benjamin, Editors, *Healers on Healing.* Los Angeles: Jeremy P. Tarcher, Inc., 1989.

Chan, Luke, *101 Miracles of Natural Healing.* Cincinatti, Ohio: Benefactor Press, 1996.

Chatwin, Bruce, *The Songlines.* New York: Penguin Books, 1987.

Chia, Mantak, *Taoist Ways to Transform Stress Into Vitality: The Inner Smile. Six Healing Sounds.* Huntington, New York: Healing Tao Books, 1985.

Chopra, Deepak, M.D., *The Book of Secrets: Unlocking the Hidden Dimensions of Your Life.* New York: Harmony Books, 2004.

Cohen, Kenneth S., The Way of Qigong, *The Art and Science of Chinese Energy Healing.* New York: Random House, Inc., 1997.

Cousins, Norman, *Anatomy of an Illness* (As Perceived by the Patient). New York: W W Norton, 1979.

Cushnir, Raphael, *Setting Your Heart on Fire: Seven Invitations to Liberate Your Life.* New York: Random House, Inc., 2003.

Dole, Elizabeth, *The Women's Book of Positive Quotations*, compiled and arranged by Leslie Ann Gibson. Minneapolis, Minnesota: Fairview Press, 2002.

Dossey, Larry, M.D. and other contributors, *The Power of Meditation and Prayer.* Carlsbad, California: Hay House, Inc., 1997.

Easwaran, Eknath, *God Makes the Rivers to Flow: Selections from the Sacred Literature of the World—Chosen for Daily Meditation.* Tomales, California: Nilgiri Press, 1991

Ellis, Richard, *Practical Reiki.* New York: Sterling Publishing Co., 1999.

Emoto, Masaru, *The Hidden Messages in Water.* Hillsboro, Oregon: Beyond Words Publishing, 2004.

Freke, Timothy, *Shamanic Wisdomkeepers: Shamanism in the Modern World. Interviews with Shamans from Different World Traditions Including Jamie Sams, Martin Prechtel and Malidoma Patrie Some.* New York: Sterling Publishing Company, 1999.

Gaynor, Mitchell L., M.D., *The Sounds of Healing: A Physician Reveals the Therapeutic Power of Sound*, Voice and Music. New York: Broadway Books, a division of Random House, Inc., 1999.

Gerber, Richard, M.D., *Vibrational Medicine: New Choices for Healing Ourselves*. New Mexico: Bear & Company, 1988.

Gibran, Kahlil, *The Prophet*. New York: Alfred A. Knopf, 1923.

Gladwell, Malcolm, *blink: The Power of Thinking Without Thinking*, New York: Time Warner Book Group, 2005.

Goldman, Jonathan, *Healing Sounds: The Power of Harmonics*. Shaftesbury, Dorset: Element Books, 1992.

Goleman, Daniel, *Emotional Intelligence: Why it Can Matter More Than IQ*. New York: Bantam Books, 1995.

Haas, Elson, M. M.D., *Staying Healthy with the Seasons*. Millbrae, California: Celestial Arts, 1981.

Hendricks, Gay, Ph.D., *Conscious Breathing: Breathwork for Health, Stress Release, and Personal Mastery*. New York: Bantam Books, 1995.

Houston, Jean, *A Passion for the Possible: A Guide to Realizing Your True Potential*. New York: HarperCollins Publishers, 1997.

Kenyon, Tom, M.A., *Brain States*. Hawaii: United States Publishing, 1994.

Keyes, Laurel Elizabeth, *Toning: The Creative Power of the Voice*. Los Angeles: DeVorss & Co., 1973.

King Jr., Martin Luther, *Random House Webster's Quotationary*. by Leonard Roy Frank, New York: Random House, Inc., 2001.

Kingston, Karen, *Clear Your Clutter with Feng Shui: Free Yourself from Physical, Mental, Emotional, and Spiritual Clutter Forever*. New York: Broadway Books, 1999.

Koestler, Arthur, *The Act of Creation*. New York: The MacMillan Co., 1964.

Kornfield, Jack, *After the Ecstasy, the Laundry: How the Heart Grows Wise on the Spiritual Path*. New York: Bantam Books, 2000.

_____, *Buddha's Little Instruction Book*. New York: Bantam Books, 1994.

Krishnamurti, quoted in *The Books in My Life*, Henry Miller. New York: New Directions, 1952.

Levey, Joel & Michelle, *Living in Balance: A Dynamic Approach for Creating Harmony & Wholeness in a Chaotic World.* Emeryville, California: Conari Press, 1998.

Linn, Denise, Space *Clearing: how to purify and create harmony in your home.* Chicago: Contemporary Books, 2000.

Loehr, Jim, and Schwartz, Tony, *The Power of Full Engagement.* New York: Free Press/Simon & Schuster, 2003.

Matthews, Caitlin, *Singing the Soul Back Home: Shamanism in Daily Life.* Boston: Element Books, Limited, 1995.

Neider, Charles, *Autobiography of Mark Twain.* New York: Perennial World Classics/ Harper, 2000.

Orloff, Judith, M.D., *Positive Energy: 10 Extraordinary Prescriptions for Transforming Fatigue, Stress & Fear Into Vibrance, Strength & Love.* New York: Harmony Books, 2004.

Purce, Jill, "Sound in Mind & Body," *Resurgence* magazine, No. 115, Mar/Apr 1986.

Santos, Daniel, D.O.M., *Luminous Essence: New Light on the Healing Body: An Alternative Healer's Story.* Wheaton, Illinois: The Theosophical Publishing House, 1997.

Simon, David, M.D., *Vital Energy: The 7 Keys to Invigorate Body, Mind & Soul.* New York: John Wiley & Sons, Inc., 2002.

Sinetar, Marsha, *The Power of Meditation and Prayer* [Michael Toms, ed.]. Carlsbad, California: Hay House, 1997.

Sky, Michael, *The Power of Emotion: Using Your Emotional Energy to Transform Your Life.* Rochester, Vermont: Bear & Company, 2002.

Stevens, Jose, Ph.D., and Stevens, Lena, *The Power Path: The Shaman's Way to Success in Business and Life.* Novato, California: New World Library, 2002.

Stone, Justin F., *T'ai Chi Chih, Joy Through Movement.* San Luis Obispo, California: Sun Publishing Company, 1974.

Veith, Ilza, trans., *The Yellow Emperor's Classic of Internal Medicine.* Berkeley, California: Univ. of California Press, 2002.

Villoldo, Alberto, Ph.D., *Shaman, Healer, Sage: How to Heal Yourself and Others with the Energy Medicine of the Americas.* New York: Harmony Books, 2000.

Warren. Rick, *The Purpose-Driven Life: What on Earth Am I Here for?* Grand Rapids, Michigan: Zondervan, 2002.

Waters, Frank, *Book of the Hopi.* New York: Penguin Books, 1963.

Wildish, Paul, *The Book of Ch'I.* Boston, Massachusetts: Tuttle Publishing, 2000.

Wolman, Richard N., *Thinking with Your Soul: Spiritual Intelligence and Why It Matters,* New York: Harmony Books, 2001.

Zambucka, Kristin, *Ano Ano: The Seed.* Oahu, Hawaii: Booklines Hawaii Ltd., 1978.

RESOURCES AND
BOOKS OF SIMILAR INTEREST

Balch, James F. M.D. and Phyllis A., C.N.C., *Prescription for Nutritional Healing, Second Edition: A Practical A-Z Reference to Drug-Free Remedies Using Vitamins, Minerals, Herbs & Food Supplements*

Balch, Phyllis A., C.N.C., *Prescription for Herbal Healing: An Easy-to-Use A-to-Z Reference to Hundreds of Common Disorders and Their Herbal Remedies*

Becker, Robert O., M.D. and Gary Selden, *The Body Electric: Electromagnetism and The Foundation of Life*

Bennett-Goleman, Tara, *Emotional Alchemy: How the Mind Can Heal the Heart*

Bruyere, Rosalyn L., *Wheels of Light, A Study of the Chakras, Volume I.* Edited by Jeanne Farrens

Chiazzari, Suzy, *The Healing Home: Creating the Perfect Place to Live with Color, Aroma, Light and Other Natural Elements*

Chopra, Deepak, M.D., *Quantum Healing: Exploring the Frontiers of Mind/Body Medicine*

_____, *Ageless Body, Timeless Mind*

_____, *How to Know God*

Desikachar, T. K. V., *The Heart of Yoga: Developing A Personal Practice*

Dossey, Larry, M.D., *The Reinvention of Medicine*

Ellis, Richard, *Practical Reiki: Focus Your Body's Energy for Deep Relaxation and Inner Peace*

Haas, Elson M., M.D. and Cameron Stauth, *The False Fat Diet*

Hale, Gail, *The Practical Encyclopedia of Feng Shui*

Hay, Louise L., *Heal Your Body A—Z: The Mental Causes for Physical Illness and the Way to Overcome Them*

_____, *Gratitude, a Way of Life*

Hunt, Valerie V., *Infinite Mind: Science of the Human Vibrations of Consciousness*

Lawless, Julia, *The Complete Illustrated Guide to Aromatherapy: A Practical Approach to the Use of Essential Oils for Health and Well-being*

Myss, Caroline, *Anatomy of the Spirit*

_____, *Spiritual Alchemy*

Narby, Jeremy, *The Cosmic Serpent: DNA and the Origins of Knowledge*

Orloff, Judith, M.D., Guide to Intuitive Healing: 5 Steps to Physical, Emotional, and Sexual Wellness

_____, *Positive Energy*

_____, *Positive Energy: 10 Extraordinary Prescriptions for Transforming Fatigue, Stress & Fear into Vibrance, Strength & Love*

Pearl, Dr. Eric, *The Reconnection: Heal Others, Heal Yourself*

Ryback, David, *Putting Emotional Intelligence to Work: Successful Leadership Is More Than IQ*

Sha, Zhi Gang, *Power Healing: The Four Keys to Energizing Your Body, Mind & Spirit*

Siegel, Bernie S., *Love, Medicine & Miracles: Lessons Learned About Self-Healing from a Surgeon's Experience with Exceptional Patients*

Some, Malidoma Patrice, *Ritual, Power, Healing and Community*

Tiwari, Maya, *A Life of Balance: The Complete Guide to Ayurvedic Nutrition & Body Types with Recipes*

Weil, Andrew, M.D., *Eating Well for Optimum Health: The Essential Guide to Food, Diet, and Nutrition*

Workman, Jennifer, M.S., R.D., *Stop Your Cravings: A Balanced Approached to Burning Fat, Increasing Energy, and Reducing Stress*

Yee, Rodney with Nina Zolotow, *Moving Toward Balance: 8 Weeks of Yoga* with Rodney Yee

AUTHOR'S NOTE

Dear Readers,

I welcome your input and ideas on the beliefs and practices presented in this book. If you have a personal story about:

- How you personally benefited from energy disciplines;
- Unique practices that work for you;
- Ways that you stay energized and balanced;
- How having a clear life purpose or identified life work has proven beneficial;
- Examples of miraculous healing;
- Examples of businesses that have offered energy practices to their employees; or
- Corporate wellness programs that have proven beneficial;

I would enjoy hearing from you. Please send an e-mail or a hard copy note to my publisher, Green Island Publishing. If you would like to receive a written response, please enclose a self-addressed envelope.

In health,

Ann

P.S. A percentage of profits from all products benefit organizations committed to improving human and planetary health.

If you want to learn more about . . .

- Executive and Individual Consulting with Ann Roulac
- Or to book Ann Roulac for a speaking engagement, in-house seminar, or motivational presentation

Please contact Ann Roulac at . . .
E-mail: ann@annroulac.com
Website: www.annroulac.com
To order the Power, Passion, and Purpose: Companion Journal, Manifest Your Desires, go to www.annroulac.com.

GREEN ISLAND PUBLISHING

Green Island Publishing is dedicated to publishing and marketing books that contribute to the health of individuals, businesses, and communities.

Please contact Green Island Publishing to find out how to:

- Order *Power, Passion, and Purpose*
- Obtain information on corporate gift programs

Green Island Publishing
709 Fifth Avenue
San Rafael, California 94901
Call toll free: 866.951.4310
E-mail: info@greenislandpublishing.com
www.greenislandpublishing.com